COURAGEOUS CHRISTIAN WOMEN

Teresa Strickler

21st Century Christian Publishing

ISBN: 978-0-89098-904-3

©2015 by 21st Century Christian

2809 12th Ave S, Nashville, TN 37204

All rights reserved.

All rights reserved. No part of this publication may be reproduced, stored in a retrieval system, or transmitted in any form or by any means—electronic, mechanical, photocopy, recording, digital, or otherwise—without the written permission of the publisher.

Unless otherwise noted Scripture quotations are from the New American Standard Bible.

Scripture taken from the NEW AMERICAN STANDARD BIBLE®,

Copyright © 1960,1962,1963,1968,1971,1972,1973,1975,1977,1995
by The Lockman Foundation. Used by permission.

Cover design by Jonathan Edelhuber

"Therefore everyone who confesses me before men, I will also confess him before my Father who is in heaven. But whoever denies me before men, I will also deny him before My Father who is in heaven."
~ Matthew 10:33 NASB

"Silence in the face of evil is itself evil: God will not hold us guiltless. Not to speak is to Speak. Not to act is to Act."
~ Dietrich Bonhoeffer

Photo by
Teresa Strickler
January 2015

DEDICATION

*For Danna Lou Skaggs Rende,
the sister who was tied to my heart,
and whose faith in me affects me every day.*

Acknowledgments

This effort would not have been possible without the gracious help of many brothers and sisters in Christ. My parents, Dan and Lutrica Skaggs, taught me through years of studies and examples at home that I was capable of reading, understanding, and applying the teachings of the Bible in my life. Memories of Bible studies with my dad, and watching my mother reading her Bible as she sat under the hair dryer will stay with me always. These memories and the lessons I learned when I was young were a great source of courage in sharing the lessons in this book with you. My parents have also been an on-going encouragement to me in speaking and teaching endeavors for ladies' classes over the years.

Numerous dear friends have encouraged me over the years to write a book. For more than thirty years, Jennifer Benshoof has told me I should do it; her belief in me quietly spurring me on. After I wrote a short article of fiction based loosely on a trial in her life many years ago, Theresa Love has also told me repeatedly to write a book. Other sisters over the years have, on occasion, said similar things.

Once I began entering words into my word processor, I began asking some special people for help. It was important to know if the thoughts I was trying to express were coherent to others. I turned first to a dear, wise brother in Christ, Larry Schales. Brother Schales desires first of all to be known as a humble, faithful servant of God. The Bible is his source of strength and wisdom. He possesses a Master's Degree in English from Texas Tech University. I knew if he felt my thoughts made sense and were in line with biblical teaching, I was on the right track.

I have also received practical help in grammar and content from Judy Lawrence and Elizabeth Blevins. Over the past years, I have forgotten some of the rules of English writing I learned in school; these two ladies not only provided sounding boards for ideas, they also critiqued my spelling and grammar. They have patiently labored through my chronic, run-on sentences, helping me remember to include periods. I do not believe I would have had the courage to submit my work to a publisher without Judy and Elizabeth. Judy's daughters, Diane Cox and Carin Linker also reviewed parts of the book, offering helpful insights on my content from younger Christian women, as well as help with grammar.

I would be deceitful and ungrateful if I neglected to give credit for biblical understanding to the men of God who I have heard preach over the years. My father shaped my understanding of the Bible as a child; Ron White has helped reverence for God's Word and understanding of God's authority expand and grow in my life as an adult. It is accurate to say this because Ron and his wife, Mary Jo, have been serving God through their work with the congregation where my husband and I attend for more than thirty-three years, which spans my adult life. His preaching and their example as a couple have consistently pointed beyond their human service toward the perfect example of Christ and love of God. There are some chapters in the book in which I have specifically referenced sermons from Ron that I am aware added to the content. It is not an exaggeration to add that there are probably other places in the book where the content has been influenced by Ron's preaching in ways I am not aware. Other speakers, such as those I have been blessed to hear at the annual Teton Family

Camp and the annual Utah Labor Day Camp have also affected my understanding of things shared in this book.

I cannot adequately give appreciation to my husband, Chuck, for his support. His example of leadership through service and his constant love are great blessings in my life. Our children, Elizabeth and Benjamin, have been great supporters in this project.

As God told Moses, it was He who made man's mouth. I have not been inspired by God, but He deserves credit for everything good that comes from me. He has used me in spite of my humanity; His power sustains me; His Word teaches me. He is worthy of all praise and honor; if you receive anything good from this book, say a prayer of thanksgiving to God.

Table of Contents

Introduction 11

CHAPTER 1
Courage to Consider the Problem............................. 13

CHAPTER 2
From Christian Culture to Counter-Culture 27

CHAPTER 3
The Feminist Mistake 41

CHAPTER 4
Source of Solutions (Part 1):
The Authority of God 53

CHAPTER 5
Source of Solutions (Part 2):
Valuing Human Life 65

CHAPTER 6
Finding Courage (Part 1):
Our Weakness, God's Strength 79

CHAPTER 7
Finding Courage (Part 2):
The Surrender & Power of Prayer 91

CHAPTER 8
Courage in Marriage:
Choose to Submit to Your Husband 103

CHAPTER 9
Courage as Mothers:
Choose to Train Your Children 117

CHAPTER 10
Courage in the Church (Part 1):
Choose to Love Your Brothers and Sisters 129

CHAPTER 11
Courage in the Church (Part 2):
Choose to Embrace Your Place 143

CHAPTER 12
Jesus, Hope of the Courageous 161

Introduction

If you are taking the time to investigate this book, thank you for your courage! I am not a big name author in the Christian book market; this is my first effort. You may be wondering who I am and what makes me think I have anything helpful to say to you.

I am an ordinary human being. I have made almost every mistake I point out in the pages of this book. I struggle with sin every day; like many people I seem to take three steps forward and two steps back in my struggles. I am of that class of Christians who believe Paul wrote Romans 7 about them. If you are looking for wisdom from a woman who has it all together, you might want to look elsewhere.

The good news for you as a reader is that this book is not a biography of me! It is not meant to highlight anything about me other than the power of God in the mind and heart of a flawed woman who depends on His grace daily. Each chapter has been an exercise in surrender as I have given my ideas about the topics over to God. I have asked Him to show me through the pages of His Word, rather than my own emotions, which direction to take. They have all turned out differently than I imagined them. I became interested in the topic of courage after several years' observation of changes in the culture of our country and in the church. One advantage of being over 50 is there are more changes to observe. God has taken my interest in politics and current events and refined it into a message I hope will reach through my generation into the future. Married or single, old or young, Christian women of all cultures can find encouragement in these pages to hold up godly priorities in their lives. I believe Christian women can shine as lights to societies wandering in darkness.

The beginning of this book is written from an American historical perspective because that is the society in which I was raised. However, the problems and degradation of culture covered in the first five chapters can be found in every culture in the world. The solutions covered in the last seven chapters are applicable to everyone.

My prayer is that readers will be awakened to the subtle changes that have been going on around them for decades; educated about the insidious power of Satan in history; provoked to careful consideration regarding the truth of the Bible; and inspired to live more deliberately a life of obedience to God, no matter the consequences. I pray that your individual courage will inspire others, and that all of us collectively can highlight the only Source of Hope for the future of humanity, Jesus Christ. I believe in this way, joyfully highlighting the wonderful, awesome truth of the Bible we can radically change our country and the world!

CHAPTER ONE

Courage to Consider the Problem

Imagine you are 45 years old. You are happily married and have three children. You live together in a nice house; you both have jobs that allow you to keep up with your debt and still spend time with your kids. It's a busy, sometimes crazy life, but you're happy. One day the girls you go to lunch with ask you what diet you are on. You are surprised that they ask because you haven't been on any diet! They point out that you haven't finished your meal the last four weeks that they've been out with you. You laugh it off, but that evening you realize you just aren't hungry very often anymore, and when you do eat, you seem to get full faster. You also notice that your pants are loose and lately you have been wearing the smaller clothes in your closet. You can't figure out how this happened without your noticing it, because weight has always been such a problem for you. You get on the scale the next morning and are shocked to see that you've lost 30 pounds! You say a prayer of thanksgiving to God for this blessing and go about your busy day.

In the next week you begin to notice that you are more tired than usual. It seems like you fall into bed every night, sleep like a log, and then drag through your day. A little voice in your head mentions the word *doctor*, but you dismiss it; the kids are having more school events this week, and you are working on a big project at work, which has to be the reason for the fatigue.

Your husband starts to express concern because he never sees you eat more than a couple of bites. Even your small clothes are getting loose, and the scale now says you have lost 50 pounds. You have been feeling dragged out and weak all the time for weeks, and in the last couple of days you are noticing that your upper abdomen seems larger than normal, and you are having pain. You know you need to go to the doctor, but you are too scared to go. Even though you are so tired and weak, you cannot sleep at night because the memories of your grandmother's and father's cancer experiences play over and over in your head. You pray and feel no relief from your concerns. Fear is your constant companion. Defensiveness is your reaction as more people express concern for you. You look in the mirror this morning and notice the whites of your eyes are actually yellow. You have had white, chalky bowel movements every day for the last week. You finally call the doctor with tears in your eyes.

After extensive testing you are diagnosed with liver cancer, stage III. You and your husband sit in the doctor's office dumbfounded as he lays out a treatment plan that includes surgery, chemotherapy, and radiation. He is cautiously optimistic about your recovery.

Sadly, many people treat their physical health in this way. Fear of what might be wrong and ignorance of what can be done keep people in denial until their conditions are so bad that drastic measures have to be taken. They immerse themselves in the external matters of their lives as long as possible, and when they cannot go on, they finally seek help. I have heard it said, "People do what they do because it works for them, and they keep doing it until it no longer works."

My sisters in Christ, I believe in the church we have done the same thing regarding the changes in our society. Those sisters old enough to remember the 1950s and '60s speak often about "the good old days" when, in spite of Woodstock and hippies, most marriages remained intact and the population of Christianity was on the rise. Younger women nod indulgently at these observations and send their children to school with concerns about how soon they will come home with assignments designed to teach them to accept homosexuality and wondering if their school will be the site of the next school shooting. And yet, young and old, we go on every day with the external and urgent matters of our lives, ignoring the signs all around us. When our minds slow down and open up, however, we cannot escape a growing unease about our society. So we pray, but nothing seems to change, and that unease grows to quiet desperation with each new disaster and crisis when it touches our lives.

One of the most common sentiments expressed by Christians regarding current events and conflicts in our culture is, "I just don't pay any attention to that stuff; I am not interested in politics, and besides, I don't have time to watch the news." Mass shootings and weather-related disasters garner prayers and attention from these tender-hearted souls, but they can spare no time or concern for the progress being made by those whose desire is to remove Christian principles from our laws, our economy, our communities, our schools, our homes, and the minds of our children. As I write these words, a large educational meeting is taking place in the state of Tennessee designed to persuade community members that they can be prosecuted under the Civil Rights Act of 1968 for speaking out against Islamic Terrorism and Shari'ah Law. Even though this is patently absurd, ignorant attendees to the meeting who don't have time to pay attention to politics may believe this propaganda and give up their right to freedom of speech by refraining from speaking out against the violent teachings of Islam. Campaigns of this sort to cow our citizens into submission to ungodliness through fear are rampant throughout our country today.

As we begin our studies, please consider these two dictionary definitions:

Politics: 1. The art or science of government, of guiding or influencing governmental policy, or of winning and holding control over a government. 2. Political affairs or business; esp.: competition between groups or individuals for power and leadership 3. Political opinions

Nationalism: devotion to national interests, unity, and independence[1]

A pervasive, dangerous misunderstanding has developed in our culture and in the brotherhood about the difference between the terms *politics* and *nationalism*. Most of us haven't even heard the term *nationalism* since World War II. That was the last time our nation came together for the cause of freedom. Men went to war, but the people at home lived with food and gas rationing and participated in drives to collect resources for the war effort. Women went to work manufacturing equipment for the effort. Prayer services were held in churches throughout the nation. When the victory was won, there was an unprecedented sense of solidarity among the citizens of our country. In WWII, the National Socialist Party, known as the Nazi's, took nationalism to an evil extreme as they sought to conquer the world. In the United States, nationalism helped stop that evil. Since WWII, every war has been an occasion for division and conflict locally as well as in the theaters of military operations. I am thankful to say that our veterans are given more respect now than the veterans of Vietnam, but there is still plenty of division in our country every time there is a war. My purpose in this discussion is not to support all wars, but to illustrate the high level of division among our populace about them.

I believe one reason the concept of nationalism has all but disappeared is the popular notion that anything to do with the nation is somehow political. People understand that politics is about power and government and the conflicts between political parties. But they do not remember that there is that concern for the well-being and unity and sovereignty of a nation called nationalism that transcends election cycles and political parties. Many Christians have gone about their lives in this country being convinced that they should enjoy the freedoms that come with being its citizens without taking responsibility for protecting those freedoms other than by engaging in military service. Average Christians insist they don't have time to pay attention to the cultural, economic, and social struggles going on in our country. At the same time, they seem to have plenty of time to keep up with shows such as "American Idol," " So You Think You Can Dance," "America's Got Talent," the latest sitcom series, or whatever sports event is available.

I believe the repression of the concept of nationalism and popular sentiment against individual Christians being involved in civil affairs have in large part paved the way for the morass of corruption that pervades our political system today and has for generations. The complacency of this nation of prosperous, free Christians since the early twentieth century as we have become more integrated to our materialistic, godless culture has allowed the growth and spread of evil not just in our political system, but in our educational system, in our churches, and in our homes. Christians have behaved as though they truly believed that without their participation the high moral standards that existed in our nation 60 years ago would magically be maintained. They have been like the frog thrown into the cold water of the soup pot who swam around happily, blissfully unaware of the slowly rising temperature of the water until it was too late, and he became frog soup.

In contrast, the Bible provides us with examples of godly women who contributed to the history of the nation of Israel. They did so in unique ways. The first example is that of the Hebrew midwives in Egypt.

Then the king of Egypt spoke to the Hebrew midwives, one of

Courage to Consider the Problem

> whom was named Shiphrah and the other was named Puah; and he said, "When you are helping the Hebrew women to give birth and see them upon the birthstool, if it is a son, then you shall put him to death; but if it is a daughter, then she shall live." But the midwives feared God, and did not do as the king of Egypt commanded them, but let the boys live. So the king of Egypt called for the midwives and said to them, "Why have you done this thing, and let the boys live?" The midwives said to Pharaoh, "Because the Hebrew women are not as the Egyptian women; for they are vigorous and give birth before the midwife can get to them." So God was good to the midwives, and the people multiplied, and became very mighty. Because the midwives feared God, He established households for them (Exodus 1:15-21).

These women recognized the evil of Pharaoh's decree. They recognized they had the ability and the responsibility to thwart his plan for the Hebrews. They stepped out because of faith, and God rewarded them.

In Exodus 2 we read of the courage of Moses' mother. First, she defied the law by keeping her son alive and hiding him for three months; second, she manipulated events so that she could have control of his teaching as a small child and then to secure him a home in Pharaoh's house God used the foresight, imagination, and creativity of this woman to establish the Liberator of Israel right under Pharaoh's nose.

When it came time for the people of God to conquer the cities of Canaan, in Joshua 2, we read of Rahab, another courageous woman who helped the nation of Israel.

> And the king of Jericho sent word to Rahab, saying, "Bring out the men who have come to you, who have entered your house, for they have come to search out all the land." But the woman had taken the two men and hidden them, and she said, "Yes, the men came to me, but I did not know where they were from. It came about when it was time to shut the gate at dark, that the men went out; I do not know where the men went.

Pursue them quickly, for you will overtake them." But she had brought them up to the roof and hidden them in the stalks of flax which she had laid in order on the roof...Now before they lay down, she came to them on the roof, and said to the men, "I know that the LORD has given you the land, and that the terror of you has fallen on us, and that all the inhabitants of the land have melted away before you. For we have heard how the LORD dried up the water of the Red Sea before you when you came out of Egypt, and what you did to the two kings of the Amorites who were beyond the Jordan, to Sihon and Og, whom you utterly destroyed. When we heard it, our hearts melted and no courage remained in any man any longer because of you; for the LORD your God, He is God in heaven above and on earth beneath. Now therefore, please swear to me by the LORD, since I have dealt kindly with you, that you also will deal kindly with my father's household, and give me a pledge of truth, and spare my father and my mother and my brothers and my sisters, with all who belong to them, and deliver our lives from death." So the men said to her, "Our life for yours if you do not tell this business of ours; and it shall come about when the LORD gives us the land that we will deal kindly and faithfully with you" (Joshua 2:3-6, 8-14).

I believe the example of Rahab should particularly touch our hearts. This account is a popular children's Bible class story, but I wonder if we appreciate the immensity and power of what this woman did. She was not a member of God's chosen people. From the perspective of an enemy, she discerned that these people would be victorious because of their God. She stepped out to help them against her king and the soldiers rifling through her house before she had spoken with the spies and before she had begged for safety for her family and herself. Perhaps this is why she is mentioned among the most faithful of the Old Testament in Hebrews 11:31.

In Judges 4 and 5 the account of two more Hebrew women who were significant in that nation's history is given. After the Hebrews had divided up the land of Canaan, they were supposed to have driven out all the other nations. However, they did not obey this command of God completely, and God used the pagan nations to test Israel. Joshua had died, and there was no single leader of the people, but a series of Judges. The Israelites fell into a cycle of disobedience to God resulting in captivity, then repentance and salvation.

One of Israel's Judges was a married woman and prophetess named Deborah. She guided the people during their captivity by Jabin, king of Canaan. After twenty years of his oppression, when the Israelites called to God, He spoke to Deborah. In Judges 4:6-9, she delivered God's command to the warrior Barak:

> Now she sent and summoned Barak the son of Abinoam from Kedesh-naphtali, and said to him, "Behold, the LORD, the God of Israel, has commanded, 'Go and march to Mount Tabor, and take with you ten thousand men from the sons of Naphtali and from the sons of Zebulun. I will draw out to you Sisera, the commander of Jabin's army, with his chariots and his many troops to the river Kishon, and I will give him into your hand.'" Then Barak said to her, "If you will go with me, then I will go; but if you will not go with me, I will not go." She said, "I will surely go with you; nevertheless, the honor shall not be yours on the journey that you are about to take, for the LORD will sell Sisera into the hands of a woman" (Judges 4:6-9).

When the armies of the Lord arrive at the river Kishon, Deborah had to verbally push Barak out to the battle.

> Deborah said to Barak, "Arise! For this is the day in which the LORD has given Sisera into your hands; behold, the LORD has gone out before you." So Barak went down from Mount Tabor with ten thousand men following him. The LORD routed Sisera and all his chariots and all his army with the edge of the sword before Barack; and Sisera alighted from his chariot and fled away on foot. But Barak pursued the chariots and the army as far as Harosheth-hagoyim, and all the army of Sisera fell by the edge of the sword; not even one was left. Now Sisera fled away on foot to the tent of Jael the wife of Heber the Kenite, for there was

peace between Jabin the king of Hazor and the house of Heber the Kenite. Jael went out to meet Sisera, and said to him, "Turn aside, my master, turn aside to me! Do not be afraid." And he turned aside to her into the tent, and she covered him with a rug. He said to her, "Please give me a little water to drink, for I am thirsty." So she opened a bottle of milk and gave him a drink; then she covered him. He said to her, "Stand in the doorway of the tent, and it shall be if anyone comes and inquires of you, and says, 'Is there anyone here?' that you shall say, 'No.'" But Jael, Heber's wife, took a tent peg and seized a hammer in her hand, and went secretly to him and drove the peg into his temple, and it went through into the ground; for he was sound asleep and exhausted. So he died. And behold, as Barak pursued Sisera, Jael came out to meet him and said to him, "Come, and I will show you the man whom you are seeking." And he entered with her, and behold Sisera was lying dead with the tent peg in his temple. So God subdued on that day Jabin the king of Canaan before the sons of Israel (Judges 4:14-23).

This victory, which freed the children of Israel from captivity, would not have been possible without the faith and courage of Deborah and Jael.

Considering Hebrew women of courage who contributed significantly to their history, Esther must be studied carefully. As a captive, this young girl found herself in the tenuous position of Queen to King Ahasuerus. Just as she was settling in to her new position as the most beloved of the King's wives, the King's servant, Haman, contrived to get the King to order the extermination of all the Jews. Esther had not revealed her heritage to the King, and though she mourned for the edict, she was also fearful that he would find out and destroy her. But Mordecai, her relative, insisted that she go and plead for the lives of her people to the King. Esther was terrified of this as entering the king's presence without permission could easily result in her death. At first she refused to go. In verse 14 of chapter 4, Mordecai's response to Esther, "...who knows whether you have not attained royalty for such a time as this?" was haunting enough to spur her to act. Her faith, humility, creativity, and charm literally saved her nation. We read the account of her dinners and speech to the king, of the destruction of Haman, and the elevation of Mordecai, but do we ever imagine ourselves taking a similarly weighted risk for even our family, much less our nation?

With the arrival of Jesus and the accounts of His teachings in the Gospels, we learn that God's kingdom is a spiritual one, and that the citizenship we need to be most concerned about is in Heaven. However, even Jesus expressed sorrow over the loss of the nation of Israel as recorded by Matthew when He cried out,

> "Jerusalem, Jerusalem, who kills the prophets and stones those who are sent to her! How often I wanted to gather your children together, the way a hen gathers her chicks under her wings, and you were unwilling. Behold, your house is being left to you desolate! For I say to you, from now on you will not see Me until you say, 'BLESSED IS HE WHO COMES IN THE NAME OF THE LORD!'" (Matthew 23:37-39)

The apostle Paul in his letter to the Roman Christians dramatically expressed his love for his Hebrew brethren when he wrote the following,

> I am telling the truth in Christ, I am not lying, my conscience testifies with me in the Holy Spirit, that I have great sorrow and unceasing grief in my heart. For I could wish that I myself were accursed, separated from Christ for the sake of my brethren, my kinsmen according to the flesh (Romans 9:1-3).

Are there any of us who love our fellow Americans that much, that we would be lost ourselves if they could be saved? When Paul wrote these words his people were captives of the Roman Empire, and he knew they would be destroyed. He knew the reasons for this physical captivity and eventual destruction were spiritual ones. He remarked that their lost state gave him constant sorrow. His inspired words in this book indicate that he was aware of not only the spiritual but the physical struggles his nation was experiencing in its final years. What was he doing about it? Did he tune out because the problem was beyond his ability to solve? Was he focused merely on saving himself and his friends? No! He obeyed the command of the Lord to preach the gospel. He used his talents for reasoning and speaking and even tent making to keep engaging whoever would listen to the truth. He eventually spoke before kings and went to Rome to appeal to Caesar.

Today we who live in America face a situation that seems to grow more desperate daily. We know it is because we as a people have turned away from God and His Word in our federal and state governments, our businesses, our communities, our schools, our churches, and our homes. Most of us do not understand how extensively Satan has been involved in the degradation of our country. This spiritual turning away has some serious physical consequences we see all around us: the bitter divisions among our people based upon race, economics, and morality; the general lack of respect and trust between people; the economic turmoil that affects every aspect of our lives and causes us to wonder what there will be for future generations; the corruption that appears to be the standard operating procedure at all levels of business and government; and, our vulnerability to those who would destroy us. What shall we as Christians do about these things? Shall we go into depression and anxiety worrying about them? Shall we allow anger over the injustices we learn about to grow into contempt for our countrymen so that we tune out everyone and everything? Once America had the undisputed title of the "Greatest Nation in the World." As Christian Americans living since WWII, we have enjoyed perhaps the greatest wealth and the most extensive freedoms of any people on earth. Now our country needs the faith, courage, creativity, ingenuity, determination, and love of Christians who are willing to recognize the talents God has given them "for such a time as this." Like

Jesus and Paul we need to love our countrymen according to the flesh enough to sacrifice for them. Like Shiphrah, Puah, Esther, Deborah, Jael, Rahab, and the mother of Moses, we need to work with our talents where God has placed us for the betterment of our people in this life as well as for eternity.

So this is not a book about "politics." Although, if there are women who have the talent and the fortitude for entering public life and service who read this book, I pray you will take the steps necessary to get involved! This is a book about appropriate nationalism and the Culture War that Christians are currently losing due to denial and ignorance. It is about our responsibility to exemplify the truth of being faithful, knowledgeable, active, submissive, hopeful Christian women. It is about spreading the truth in our families and communities. As a Christian **you** have the answers to the ills that plague our nation. May the information in this book give you the courage to step out in your life and share those answers by your words and your example.

CHAPTER ONE **Questions for Discussion**

1. If you have experienced a medical situation similar to the one described at the beginning of this chapter, was your relief at learning the diagnosis and beginning the treatment plan greater or less than the fear you had before you went to the doctor?
2. How is the culture in which you now live different from the one you knew as a child?
3. Discuss your thoughts on how hopeful you are for the future of the community where you live, the state, the country, and the world.
4. Given the irritations Christians experience daily from interacting with people who do not share our belief in following the Bible, and describe your reaction to the idea of loving our fellow citizens in the way Paul expressed loving his fellow Jews in Romans 9.

5. Based on this study, explain your thoughts on whether nationalism is a biblical concept.

6. If laws were passed in your country that went directly against the commands of God, can you imagine yourself disobeying them?

Reference

1. Merriam-Webster's Dictionary AND Thesaurus, Copyright 2007, by Merriam-Webster, Incorporated, MADE IN THE UNITED STATES OF AMERICA.

CHAPTER TWO

From Christian Culture to Counter-Culture

In the first chapter we considered some examples of God's people engaging in brave behaviors because of nationalism. In this chapter we will learn how the principles of Christianity have gone from being the underpinnings of the United States of America to being a literal "counter-culture" here.

The best place to begin addressing the foundations of our nation is to look at the *Declaration of Independence*. This document was ratified on July 4, 1776, but knowledge of what the document contains and appreciation for the risk involved in ratifying it is on the decline among our people.

> When in the Course of human events, it becomes necessary for one people to dissolve the political bands which have connected them with another, and to assume among the powers of the earth, the separate and equal station to which the Laws of Nature and of Nature's God entitles them, a decent respect to the opinions of mankind requires that they should declare the causes which impel them to the separation.

The purpose of this document was to give the King of England notice that the colonies, represented by the men who signed it, were severing ties with England to become their own nation. Notice in this opening passage that it was the belief of these men that the "Laws of Nature and of Nature's God" entitled them to take this action.

> We hold these truths to be self-evident, that all men are created equal, that they are endowed by their Creator with certain unalienable Rights; that among these are Life, Liberty, and the pursuit of Happiness.

Although the Declaration is not as well-known as it used to be, most Americans have a passing familiarity with this passage. The concepts of Natural Law and Unalienable Rights originating from a Creator were not born with the American colonists. The Roman philosopher Marcus Tullius Cicero (106-43 B.C.) first discussed the necessary elements of an enduring society in his 47 B.C. work, *Republic*. The men we refer to as the Founding Fathers studied his philosophies carefully as they sought to create a new country.[5]

Cicero's observations of the world and of men led him to reason that the world was created, and that the Creator of the world had given man the gift of reason, the ability to figure out the existence of design and Designer, and to learn the law of the world. This Cicero referred to as "True Law." His statement of this true law was critical to the understanding of the founders of our nation.[5]

> True law is right reason in agreement with nature; it is of universal application, unchanging and ever-lasting; it summons to duty by its commands, and averts from wrongdoing by its prohibitions....It is a sin to try to alter this law, nor is it allowable to repeal any part of it, and it is impossible to abolish it entirely. We cannot be freed from its obligations by senate or people, and we need not look outside ourselves for an expounder or interpreter of it. And there will not be different laws at Rome and at Athens, or different laws now and in the future, but one eternal and unchangeable law will be valid for all nations and all times, and there will be one master and ruler, that is God, over us all, for He is the author of this law, its promulgator, and its enforcing judge. Whoever is disobedient is fleeing from himself and denying his human nature, and by reason of this very fact he will suffer the worst punishment.[5]

Cicero lived and died before Jesus ever walked the earth; he was Roman, of the race that held the Jews in captivity. Yet he had been able to discern the existence of the eternal God and His laws, just as we read in Romans 1 is possible through observation of what has been made.

The *Declaration of Independence* ends with the following passage:

> We, therefore, the Representatives of the United States of America, in General Congress, Assembled, appealing to the Supreme Judge of the world for the rectitude of our intentions, do, in the Name, and by the Authority of the good People of these Colonies, solemnly publish and declare, That these United Colonies are, and of Right ought to be Free and Independent States;...And for the support of this Declaration, with a firm reliance on the protection of divine Providence, we mutually pledge to each other our Lives, our Fortunes, and our sacred Honor.

The 56 men who signed this document did not do so lightly. What they were doing was committing treason. Their "firm reliance on the protection of divine Providence," combined with their conviction that their rights came from God, gave them the courage they needed to take this action. Once this document was signed, the rag-tag colonists battled the greatest military in the known world for five bloody years, finally achieving their goal in March 1781.[5]

However, the colonists, having finally won their independence were reluctant to once again place themselves in subjection to any government. By 1787 the fledgling country was struggling economically and socially because of the splintered nature of the state governments. Currencies and laws varied from state to state, and larger countries took advantage of these issues to exploit businesses. Behind the scenes, for many years, some special men, commonly referred to as "Founding Fathers," had been striving to perfect random ideas into a radically different form of government. Three of these men, John Jay, James Madison, and Alexander Hamilton began in early 1787 to publish their ideas in what is now known as "The Federalist Papers." These men did not even agree with one another on everything, but they agreed that for the United States to remain and flourish it needed a document, a Constitution. In the summer of 1787 representatives from the states came together and in the fall, September 17, 1787, the *Constitution of the United States* was signed by the delegates of the first Constitutional Convention.[5]

The Constitution, though drafted by men who did not agree on details, was based upon their agreement with 28 major principles. What is fascinating to the modern Bible student who also enjoys history is how many of those principles are in harmony with the Bible. The first five of these principles deal directly with the necessity of faith in God: These are natural law; virtue among the people; religion's role; the Creator's role; and all men created equal. Some other principles include self-government; avoiding alliances; importance of the family; and avoiding debt. An in-depth study of the underpinnings of the Constitution and those who wrote it leaves the student with confidence that our Founding Fathers intended this country to be based on Christian principles.[4]

However, the phrase most often thrown at Christians regarding the Constitution is "separation of church and state." Since 1962 when prayer was successfully removed from our public schools, this mantra has been used with nearly absolute impunity. Our ignorance of the truth of the intent of our founders has left us vulnerable to false arguments and blunted the edge of our courage to stand for the truth of God's Word.

When the Pilgrims arrived on this continent in the 1600s one of the things they were getting away from was the state-sponsored religion of Britain. As the colonies became states and then a country, one of the great concerns was that religion would again be forced on the citizens by the government. The first of the ten amendments of the Constitution was designed specifically to prevent this. "Congress shall make no law establishing religion..." stated that the government could not establish any religion of which its citizens would be *forced* to be members. The second phrase of this amendment has not been quoted nearly as often, "...or prohibiting the exercise thereof." The authors of this document and those who signed it expected that religion would be part of American life and desired to forbid the government from infringing on the exercise of faith.[1]

So, where does this "separation of church and state" concept come from? This phrase was used in a letter Thomas Jefferson wrote to a group of Baptist believers in Danbury, Connecticut in January 1802. These citizens were concerned that by including protection for religion in the Constitution the framers had left open the opportunity for a State religion. This was Mr. Jefferson's reply to their apprehension:

> Believing with you that religion is a matter which lies solely between man and his God, ...I contemplate with sovereign reverence that act that the whole American people which declared that their legislature should "make no law respecting an establishment of religion or prohibiting the free exercise thereof," thus building a wall of separation between Church and State.[1]

The phrase "separation of church and state" does not appear anywhere in the First Amendment. Clearly Mr. Jefferson's letter was intended to reassure these people that they would not face religion imposed upon them by the state. Even this brief overview of *The Declaration of Independence* and *The Constitution of the United States* and *Bill of Rights* reveals the intention that the United States would exist as a Christian nation. We can be thankful to God for this remarkable nation in which we have enjoyed such religious freedom.[1]

As he seeks to twist all good things, however, Satan was not long delayed in striving to twist what was intended to be a light in a dark world. He has had great success in using human tools for transforming our society from one dominated by a Christian mindset to one dominated by dark forces, where truth is suppressed and each generation is more ignorant of truth than the one before. There is a history to this movement as well, and its broad scope is a stunning example of Satan's ingenuity. I believe a brief survey of facets of this movement is important for us as Christians to motivate us toward the renewal and revival of practice of our Christian faith and outreach to our country.

In 1847, fewer than one hundred years after our nation was established, across the world another movement became public, communism. With the publishing of *The Communist Manifesto*, Karl Marx and his financier/partner Friedrich Engels burst upon the international scene. Karl Marx once declared,

> "My purpose in life is to dethrone God and destroy capitalism."[6]

His Manifesto was born after years of Marx's indoctrination in anti-God philosophies reaching as far back as Epicurus the materialist and Prometheus who said, "In one word—I hate all the gods!" This Manifesto declared to the world the steps for creating a communist society:

> 1. The overthrow of capitalism, 2. The abolition of private property, 3. The elimination of the family as a social unit, 4. The abolition of all classes, 5. The overthrow of all governments, and 6. The establishment of a communist order with communal ownership of property in a classless, stateless society.[6]

In 1891, in a small town on one of the islands of Italy a child was born. His name was Antonio Gramsci. Though Karl Marx was the originator of revolutionary communism, Gramsci expanded on Marx's philosophies and first publicized methods of spreading communistic philosophies without military revolution. In many ways his insidious philosophies have proven to be more harmful to godly, freedom-loving people than the blatant teachings of

Karl Marx. Mr. Gramsci had observed the turbulence of political revolution and the temporary nature of its success. He believed and taught that the way for communism to succeed was to take on the values of the *bourgeois* (normal people) and change them over time. He believed that if one could successfully change the beliefs and ideas of the dominant group in a culture, political revolution could take place without violence. Mr. Gramsci wrote these principles in almost three thousand pages of notebooks between 1925 and 1937 after he was put in prison by Mussolini. He discussed how through formal and informal education a society could be convinced to view communistic principles as "common sense." He advocated for all those who are considered "intellectuals" in their various fields whether "managers, civil servants, clergy, professors, teachers, technicians, scientists, lawyers, and doctors" to assist in instructing the populace to accept the evolution of their culture away from one that supports individuality and freedom and into one that is communal in nature. His works were published in English in the 1970s.[7]

Just prior to Gramsci's death in 1937, a book was published in 1932 entitled, *Toward Soviet America*. The book was designed to dispel "capitalist lies about communism and to expose the evils of capitalism; it also included a specific plan for implementing socialism and fascism in the United States. The plan included freeing women from the slavery of life at home and sexual taboos imposed by churches and moralists, no-fault divorce, and the removal of stigma of having children out of wedlock. Childcare and feeding would be taken over by the government to free the woman from these duties so that she might work. The book rails against "Superstitious dolts who will satisfy themselves with a promise of a paradise after death as a substitute for a decent life here on earth" in the section of the plan for improving the lot of children in America. Promising that past beliefs would be replaced in Soviet America with scientific materialistic philosophy, the plan calls for "all education to be coordinated under a National Department of Education with state and local branches." All religious and patriotic elements of education would be removed, replaced with materialism, internationalism, and the ethics of socialism. All religious schools would be removed, and it would be against the law to teach minor children religion.[3]

In 2001, at a school in Superior, Wisconsin, students began to recite the following instead of the Pledge of Allegiance: "I Pledge Allegiance to the World; To Care for Earth, Sea, and Air; To Honor Every Living Thing; With Peace and Justice Everywhere."[2]

With the fall of Soviet Communism in 1989, most of us believed that the threat to our nation from that quarter was over. We believed we had won the "Cold War," but many did not recognize the growing corruption already at work in our country. As of 2010, fewer than 10 percent of publicly educated children left school with a firm belief in absolute right and wrong. Also as of that year, 85 percent of children who were raised with a Southern Baptist faith left the church once they left home. Since 1950, organizations have been forming to push for rights for homosexuals, and today we have the legalization of homosexual marriage in several of our states.[2]

On the media front our nation has been bombarded for generations by increasing amounts of ugliness, barbarism, and hopelessness. It turns out this is also by design. When the Bolshevik Revolution failed to spread throughout Europe and into the United States, a Hungarian aristocrat named Georg Lukacs became part of the Frankfurt School. This was the euphemistic name for a communist think tank whose purpose was to discern how to successfully defeat the Western way of life and replace it with communism. His contribution in part is as follows:

> Any political movements capable of bringing Bolshevism to the West would have to be demonic and possess the religious power which is capable of filling the entire soul; a power that

characterized primitive Christianity. However, this could only succeed when the individual no longer believes his actions are determined by personal destiny, but the destiny of the community, in a world that has been abandoned by God.[8]

Lukacs contended that the Western belief in the individual as being created by God and therefore having direct access to God and dominion over nature had to be destroyed in order for this new philosophy to take hold. The job of the Frankfurt school, then, became two-fold: "to undermine the Judeo-Christian legacy through an abolition of culture; and second, to determine new cultural forms which would increase the alienation of the population, thus creating a new barbarism."[8]

The intricacies of this agenda reach back to the account of creation and make man above good and evil, remove order and standards in favor of chaos theory, which is taught in our universities today as professional business practice. Art becomes the imitation of chaos and destruction rather than order and beauty. All that is uplifting must be destroyed, whether art, literature, or music. The goal of performance becomes to bemuse and anger the audience. Adherents to this philosophy were influential in the beginning of radio and television programming. They studied human nature carefully and tailored programming to addicting audiences with the question "what happens next?" in fiction and news coverage.

> "The Frankfurt School's most important breakthrough consists in the realization that their monstrous theories could become dominant in the culture, as a result of the changes in society by...the age of mechanical reproduction of art."[8]

Their studies of human nature combined with their ungodly desires to dominate our people led to the creation of the first modern public opinion poll studies categorizing people without regard for the individuals' ability to think for themselves. This has led to our current state of political affairs where entire campaigns are based on polls. And our populace, addicted to news coverage and faithful to the opinions of academic "experts," has followed like sheep.[8]

In 1955, Herbert Marcuse, one of the members of the Frankfurt School published the book *Eros and Civilization*, funded by the Rockefeller Foundation. The foundation was one of the major American supporters of the Frankfurt School. This book is known as the "founding document" of the 1960s counter-culture. Marcuse believed that the erotic, sensuous side of man had to be liberated in order to free him from what he termed "A comfortable, smooth, reasonable, democratic unfreedom...in advanced industrial civilization, a token of technical progress."[8]

Marcuse's theory was an underlying part of Sigmund Freud's philosophies but was overtly emphasized by modern philosophers such as Wilhelm Reich and Carl Jung. We typically look back at the drug culture and immorality of the '60s and are reminded of their push for free love and their animosity for the traditional family. But it was in that time that our culture began to accept the objectifying of people determined by their natures. This opened the door for the homosexual movement as people engaged in that behavior began to argue that they were born that way and were a slave to their nature. As a culture we gave up on the idea that individuals were individually gifted and capable of changing the world around them for good. People became important for their gender or their color or their sexual orientation, as mentioned above. It was in this atmosphere that the civil rights movement became the "Black Power" and "Feminism" movements.[8]

Since the 1960s freedom revolution, our culture has continued to chase sensuality, chaos, and destruction with ever greater enthusiasm. Our universities are dominated by adherents to the philosophies of Marcuse and other adherents to the Frankfurt School, and this think tank is revered openly in the halls of higher learning. One of these philosophies which is popularly taught and implemented daily in our culture is "repressive toleration." This term refers to the "tolerance for movements from the left, but intolerance for movements from the right." Professor Cornell West of Princeton University, one of the most famous professors in the country, openly states that his philosophical theories come from Georg Lukacs.[8]

The information I have shared in this chapter about the Frankfurt School came from an article published in 1992. The article ends in part this way:

> The principles through which Western Judeo-Christian civilization was built, are now no longer dominant in our society; they exist only as a kind of underground resistance movement. If that resistance is ultimately submerged, then the civilization will not survive-and...the collapse of Western civilization will very likely take the rest of the world with it to Hell. The way out is to create a Renaissance. A renaissance means, to start again; to discard the evil, and the inhuman, and just plain stupid, and to go back, hundreds or thousands of years, to the ideas which allow humanity to grow in freedom and goodness. ...it depends on seemingly ordinary people who will defend the divine spark of reason in themselves, and tolerate no less in others. Given the successes of the Frankfurt School and its New Dark Age sponsors, these ordinary individuals, with their belief in reason and the difference between right and wrong, will be "unpopular." But, no really good idea was ever popular, in the beginning.[8]

Although the information in this text seems extensive and varied, it does not begin to scratch the surface of the tools Satan has used since the 19th century to attack and demoralize our nation. He has used organizations, individuals, and both political parties to reach his objective. It is easy to get caught up in blame and anger and discouragement over these facts as one researches them. However, as Christians we are not taught to do so.

For as devious as all of these schemes have been, these are only false copies of God's plan. God thought first of the incremental indoctrination at all levels of society! The difference is that God's news is good news! We have the truth of the gospel, the plan of salvation, God's plan for man, all in the Bible. Consider these important words we have from Jesus:

> "You are the salt of the earth; but if the salt has become tasteless, how can it be made salty again? It is no longer good for anything, except to be thrown out and trampled underfoot by men. You are the light of the world. A city set on a hill cannot be hidden; nor does anyone light a lamp and put it under a basket, but on the lampstand, and it gives light to all who are in the house. Let your light shine before men in such a way that they see your good works, and glorify your Father who is in heaven." (Matthew 5:13-16)

Jesus also spoke these words to believers.

> "What I tell you in the darkness, speak in the light; and what you hear whispered in your ear, proclaim upon the housetops. Do not fear those who kill the body but are unable to kill the soul; but rather fear Him who is able to destroy both soul and body in hell. Are not two sparrows sold for a cent? And yet not one of them will fall to the ground apart from your Father. But the very hairs of your head are all numbered. So do not fear; you are more valuable than many sparrows. Therefore everyone who confesses Me before men, I will also confess him before My Father who is in heaven. But whoever denies Me before men, I will also deny him before My Father who is in heaven." (Matthew 10:27-33)

Let us commit our minds to learning anew the plan of God for the Christian life. Let us commit our hearts again to obedience and sacrifice for the One who gave everything for us. Let us commit our energies to spreading the truth and beauty and order of Christianity to our families and communities.

CHAPTER TWO **Questions for Discussion**

1. If you have never read the entire Declaration of Independence, find a copy and read it. After reading that document, how do

your impressions of the content compare with those who say it was written by men who did not believe in God?

2. The philosopher Cicero believed that rulers who did not rule according to God's laws were in danger of punishment. What would he think of the leaders of the United States today?

3. After learning that the origin of the phrase "separation of church and state" from Thomas Jefferson has been obscured so effectively that the Supreme Court in 1962 voted to ban open prayer in schools, are you curious about other "truths"' you have learned about the United States?

4. In Hosea 4:6 in the prophet's warning to God's people he quotes, "My people are destroyed by lack of knowledge… " After reading this chapter, explain how that verse might apply to Christians in the United States and around the world. Discuss whether you believe the knowledge we need is spiritual, secular, or both.

5. A common reaction to negative information about history and politics is hopelessness, leading to anger and isolation as we push the "off" button and tune out. Brainstorm with the class what Matthew 5:13-16 and Matthew 10:27-33 reveal to us about how God wants Christians to respond to the realities in the world around us.

References

1. Barton, David, 2009. Separation of Church and State: What the Founders Meant. Wallbuilders, Aledo, Texas, United States.
2. Curtis Bowers, 2010. Agenda: Grinding America down. Idaho, United States.
3. Foster, W.Z, 1932. Toward Soviet America. Reprinted 2012 Forgotten Books, Lexington, Kentucky, United States.
4. Skousen, W. C., 2006. The 5000 Year Leap: A Miracle that Changed the World. National Center for Constitutional Studies, Malta, Idaho, United States.
5. Skousen, W.C., 1985. The Making of America: the Substance and Meaning of the Constitution. The National Center for Constitutional Studies, Malta, Idaho, United States.
6. Skousen, W.C., 2012. The Naked Communist. Ensign Publishing Company, Riverton, Utah, United States.
7. (http://inged.org/mobi/antonio-gramsci-schooling-and-education/) accessed August 29, 2013. Antonio Gramsci, schooling and education.

8. (http://www.schillerinstitute.org/fid_91-96/921_frankfurt.html) accessed August 29,2013. Minnicino, Michael, The New Dark Age: the Frankfurt school and political correctness. Reprinted from the Winter 1992 issue of Fidelio Magazine.

CHAPTER THREE

The Feminist Mistake

At the 2013 graduation of cadets from West Point, the commencement address included a lament on the scourge that is sexual assaults on women in the military. When I heard about this on MSNBC News, I thought it was unusual that such a subject would be covered at a ceremony that is a celebration of achievement and encouragement for students to go out and conquer the world. The specific account of assault that the network covered in conjunction with this event was disturbing. A female cadet had been invited by a male colleague back to his room after work. She had gone with him and was surprised when he attempted to kiss her. The kiss became a rape. She had to leave West Point after this event, and the man involved finished his program and graduated. When asked by the reporter how she felt about this, she replied, "sad and scared."

As disturbing as any sexual assault is, what truly bothered me about this event was the tragic misinformation that may have been the background that set these people up for this devastating, evil event. Since Elizabeth Cady Stanton first presented her "Declaration of Sentiments" at the Seneca Falls Convention in 1848, the feminist movement has been alive and growing in this country.[1] Though I would not argue with some of the independence women have gained over the last 150 years, the basic tenet of feminism, that excepting some increasingly inconvenient organs, men and women are exactly the same, has caused much damage to our society. The social customs that in ages past educated young women that it was inappropriate to be alone with a man not her husband were swept away as "Victorian" or "paranoid." We have educated our children that there is no difference between the sexes. The realities of sexual drive in men have not been taught, rather they have been ridiculed. Men have been stripped of their masculinity, and it has been demanded of them that they accept the presence of women who are not their wives in every corner of their lives. Women expect to be able to wear as little clothing as they desire in close quarters with men and have no repercussions because they expect men to perceive them as "one of the guys" or because they enjoy the power they have over men in modern culture.

And so we have men and women training together for the military at West Point. I am certain that this female cadet had no intention of arousing or leading on the upper classman who assaulted her. I am sure she was dressed in a way that was within military code. I am sure that in no way had she consciously "asked" to be raped. She believed she was a sexless human being with another sexless human being and thought nothing of going to his room alone. His assault on her obviously reveals he had a different perception of the relationship as well as her consent to go to his room. She was enjoying her absolute equality; he viewed her as an object for his use.

This sad situation leaves me wondering when, or if, common sense will ever return in our culture. We have generations of ignorant people around us who have bought into godless, evolutionary concepts and have set up unrealistic expectations of men and women. Our media has glorified the "one-night stand" and "friends with benefits" until our junior high aged children text one another to meet in parking lots for sex with no more meaning than a kiss. The majority of movies or television programs do not offer a conventional, two-parent, heterosexual marriage and family for our children to admire. According to the Centers for Disease Control 2011 report on sexually transmitted diseases in our country, there are twenty million new cases of STDs in the U.S. every year. Treating STDs in our country costs approximately $17 billion a year. The data relating to young people is depressing. The report says that "Young people represent 25% of the sexually experienced population in the United States, but account for nearly half of the new sexually transmitted diseases."[2]

Another result of the feminist movement in our country has been the diminishing and demeaning of the influence of men in our culture. This systematic effort has been alive and well in our schools, colleges, entertainment, and government and has resulted in a decline in young men going to college, starting careers, and getting married. Since the 1970s, men have been stereotyped as ignorant, unemotional, clumsy, and arrogant buffoons who were meant to be kept in line by the women in their lives. They were supposed to go to work to pay the family bills, come home early enough to watch the kids so their wives could have their "me time," but otherwise stay out of the way of the family. In the twenty-first century they have been relegated to the man cave, whether it is a solitary room in the basement or the whole garage. Otherwise they are to have no opinion regarding running the home or raising the children. In the event of a divorce, the children are awarded to the mother by default, with the husband being enslaved to child support payments that keep him just above bankruptcy for the duration of the children's minority. What the feminists did not count on was that eventually the men would wise up to their role in society as domestic slaves and drop out of the game before it got started.

> "...In 1970, 80% of 25 to 29-year-old men were married; in 2007, only about 40% of them were. In 1970, 85% of 30- to 34-year-old men were married; in 2007, only 60% of them were." "The

US marriage rate has dipped 40% over the past four decades, to its lowest point ever. There are many plausible explanations for this trend, but one of the least mentioned is the American men, in the face of a family court system which is hopelessly stacked against them, have subconsciously launched a marriage strike."[3]

Young men have also been withdrawing from higher education in disturbing numbers.

"Between 1975 and 2006, the percentage of women with at least a college degree increased from 18.6% to 34.2%. Men barely budged: their numbers went from 26.8% to 27.9%."[3]

This lack of interest in higher education could have to do with the fact that the elementary and secondary education systems have been designed to favor girls and reprogram the boyishness out of boys. In our schools boys' needs and masculine traits are looked down on, and gender experts at prestigious universities like Harvard believe they need to be led away from "conventional maleness." The active, rambunctious boy is taught that he is uncivilized and made to feel out of place, or he is diagnosed with autism or ADHD. By the time he finishes high school, if he does, he has no plans to go further in education which he may find boring, and winds up taking low-paying jobs that cannot support himself much less a family. Since 1969 the median wage of the American male has decreased by $13,000 a year, a reduction of 28%.[3]

As an amateur observer of our culture for the last twenty years, I have observed a disturbing trend: men between the ages of 17 and 30 committing mass murder. They are blowing up buildings and schools and shooting up theaters. They are living in their parents' basements playing video games or watching TV. Some of them are using technology for criminal activities such as identity theft while others are addicted to porn. The normal impulses created in young men that used to lead them to educate themselves and take wives and build families are still there, but so many of today's young men do not know what to do with these impulses. Even faithful Christian families are finding themselves with sons who never seem to "launch" into adulthood either as husbands and fathers or as servants in the church.

And what about our daughters; how has the proliferation of the feminist doctrine changed the culture for them? The story at the beginning of this section illustrates an individual case of the results in the attitude that women and men can do everything equally as well. It is a naïve mistake, however, to believe that feminism stops with equality between men and women. The modern feminist looks down on men as second-class citizens. She has been taught from elementary school that not only is she no different than a man and can do whatever he can, but also she has been taught that she does not need a man. She has been taught that she is special, beautiful, intelligent, talented, and that she must develop all of her attributes to their fullest or she is not a complete, fulfilled person. A girl who does not seek education and career as her first priority in life is labeled as having poor self-esteem. Career women can make no greater mistake than to imply that a relationship with a man is at the center of her life. There is no middle ground, no room at the top of the career ladder for husband and family. Society's daughters leave home for college and career and a life fulfilling all their greatest desires. If they decide at some point they want a child, they can have in-vitro fertilization. But most of them do not desire to have children. Having a family is not on the list of goals for these modern young women.

One consequence of the attitudes and lives of modern young men and women who live to fulfill their destinies, great or small, is many of them never learn the adult virtues of sacrifice for others or the agape love of the Bible. They are busy loving themselves and have no room for anyone else. They leave the church, that antiquated institution which does not appreciate them or fill their needs; and they leave God, who is a fairytale according to everything they have been taught at school.

Our congregations are aging and shrinking. There are fewer weddings than there are funerals. There are almost as many divorces as there are weddings. Our Bible classes are shrinking. More of our members are falling away as families, in part, I believe because the women in those families are in charge of the activities in which the family will engage. These mothers want to see their children excel in school or sports, so that is where the family spends their time. They are either busy at the time for all church services, or they are tired from the hectic week and just cannot find the energy to make it to church. The fathers in these families have abdicated their God-given authority to the wives in the name of peace.

If we want the morality of our culture to improve, if we want our sons to become strong, righteous men living as servants of God and leaders of families, if we want our daughters to be willing to become faithful Christian wives and mothers, we have to begin with the intentions and actions of the Creator, Master of our universe. We must go back to the Bible. As women who enjoy the most freedoms of any on earth, we must choose joyfully to subject ourselves to God. This deliberate choice includes returning to respect for our husbands, fathers, and church leadership in our homes, families and culture. It also includes making time in our busy lives for teaching God's plan in our homes and children's Bible classes in an effort to change our culture by training those who will make up that culture after us.

As we begin to consider these things, I would like you to draw the following image in your mind. A man and woman are walking along a beach at dusk. The ocean is softly lapping at the shore, with a few stars in the sky, and there is a light breeze. The couple stops and watches as the sun dips below the waves; and then the man turns to the woman, lifts her chin to him and kisses her. Their embrace is long and tender. Afterward they continue walking down the beach hand-in-hand until you cannot see them anymore. Few hearts could avoid feeling warmed or even a little envious of this couple. But my question for you reader is how would you feel watching this scene being played out by a couple in their late 70s? Is your first response one of distaste or do you think to yourself, "Isn't that cute!" or something like that?

If imagining such a romantic scene occurring between two people of advanced age makes you uncomfortable, it is probably because you, like many in our society, have been influenced to a degree by worldly definitions of satisfying romantic relationships and their place in our lives. Since before the time of Shakespeare, literature, theatre, and music have indoctrinated their consumers with the idea that romance belongs to the beautiful and young. The assumption for many years has been that romance is the most important, if not the only reason for a man and woman to be together, and that if there is no romance the relationship should end.

In the Bible we learn of God's plan for men and women and relationships. Beginning with Adam and Eve, who were created for one another, God designed men and women to complete one another. Consider the beautiful account of the first wedding.

> Then the LORD God said, "It is not good for the man to be alone; I will make him a helper suitable for him." Out of the ground the LORD God formed every beast of the field and every bird of the sky, and brought them to the man to see what he would call them; and whatever the man called a living creature, that was its name. The man gave names to all the cattle, and to the birds of the sky, and to every beast of the field, but for Adam there was not found a helper suitable for him. So the LORD God caused a deep sleep to fall upon the man, and he slept; then He took one of his ribs and closed up the flesh at that place. The LORD God fashioned into a woman the rib which He had taken from the man, and brought her to the man. The man said, "This is now bone of my bones, and flesh of my flesh; she shall be called

The Feminist Mistake

> Woman, because she was taken out of Man." For this reason a man shall leave his father and his mother, and be joined to his wife; and they shall become one flesh (Genesis 2:18-24).

Notice, God did not make another man for Adam to be with, and there were no animals fit to be his partner. Only the woman was suitable to be his closest companion, and only one woman was created to fulfill this need.

Nowhere in these first Scriptures do we see a requirement that the man and woman "fall in love" in order to become one flesh and stay together for their lifetimes. Genesis 24, the chapter which tells the story of how Isaac and Rebekah became husband and wife, shows a process foreign to any love story you will see in the movies, read about in a secular book, or hear about in a song. This was an arranged marriage and not even arranged by the parents. Abraham tasked his most trusted servant to go back to his homeland and his relatives to find a wife for his son. Isaac had no say in this, and there is evidence that he was over 40 years old at this time! This servant was a godly man and depended on God to give him success in his search. He was in a strange land and had no knowledge of Abraham's family. God led him straight to Rebekah after his prayer. Abraham had told his servant that if the woman refused to come he would be free of the oath he had made to find this wife for Isaac. Once Rebekah learned who he was, she took him home to her family. The servant made known his errand to bring back a wife for Isaac. At this time the choice was with the father, Laban. He immediately agreed to this arranged marriage. Rebekah did not argue; she obeyed her father and left with Abraham's servant the next morning. When they returned to Abraham and Isaac, the two were immediately married.

> Then Isaac brought her into his mother Sarah's tent, and he took Rebekah, and she became his wife and he loved her; thus Isaac was comforted after his mother's death (Genesis 24:67).

This account is not at all meant to imply that God did not intend husbands and wives to enjoy romance with one another! Consider this romantic Scripture:

> Let your fountain be blessed, and rejoice in the wife of your youth. As a loving hind and a graceful doe, let her breasts satisfy you at all times; be exhilarated always with her love (Proverbs 5:18-19).

The book of Song of Solomon describes in even more detail the love and exhilaration between a husband and wife.

God's plan for men and women includes far more than meeting the human need for sexual expression. In Ephesians 5:22-33 we learn that the marriage relationship is a metaphor for the relationship between Christ and His church. Reading that passage we see that the man is commanded to show sacrificial love for his wife, as Christ laid down His physical life for the church. Reciprocating that, the wife is to show sacrificial love by submitting her will in obedience to that of her husband, as Christ's church submits to His will in everything. When a man and a woman come to a marriage with the intention to follow God's plan for each role, they can truly become the "one flesh" God described in Genesis. The prior commitment the bride and groom have made to be obedient to the Lord gives them the power to surrender themselves to one another as husband and wife.

> Some Pharisees came to Jesus, testing Him and asking, "Is it lawful for a man to divorce his wife for any reason at all?" And He answered and said, "Have you not read that He who created them from the beginning MADE THEM MALE AND FEMALE, and said, 'FOR THIS REASON A MAN SHALL LEAVE HIS FATHER AND MOTHER AND BE JOINED TO HIS WIFE, AND BE TWO SHALL BECOME ONE FLESH'? So they are no longer two, but one flesh. What therefore God has joined together, let no man separate" (Matthew 19:3-6).

This Scripture is so important to our study that here is the parallel reading in Mark:

> Some Pharisees came up to Jesus, testing Him, and began to question Him whether it was lawful for a man to divorce a wife. And He answered and said to them, "What did Moses command you?" They said, "Moses permitted a man TO WRITE A CERTIFICATE OF DIVORCE AND SEND HER AWAY." But Jesus said to them, "Because of your hardness of heart he wrote you this commandment. But from the beginning of creation, God MADE THEM MALE AND FEMALE. FOR THIS REASON A MAN SHALL LEAVE HIS FATHER AND MOTHER, AND THE TWO SHALL BECOME ONE FLESH; so they are no longer two but one flesh. What therefore God has joined together, let no man separate" (Mark 10:2-9).

Jesus made it clear that the marriage relationship was created and intended by God to be between one man and one woman and to last to the end of life on this earth.

Going back to our elderly couple on the beach, if we imagine they are faithful Christians who have been married to one another for many decades, we can see that their display of affection is not meant to be a "cute" or abnormal display of shallow affection. It is the well-earned celebration by two people of the blessing God has given them in faithful companionship throughout the up and down times of life. Such a display ought to provoke awe and respect in us all, rather than condescension.

As parents of young men and women, we must be courageously responsible to teach our children God's true intention for love and marriage. They need to learn that God created men and women to complete one another. We need to begin when they are young to help them have the courage they are going to need to go against the pressures of the culture around them. We need to help them prepare to be strong Christians, happy in the role God has given them. We also need to pray for God to provide them with Christian spouses who will work as partners with them to get to heaven.

CHAPTER THREE **Questions for Discussion**

1. Share any examples you have observed of the "war on men" or boys in your community. If you cannot think of any examples, are you willing to consider the idea that such a war exists?
2. Consider the young people you know between the ages of 14 and 31. How many of the young men want to eventually marry and father children? How many of the young women have that desire?
3. Reflect on the account of Rebekah in Genesis 24. By today's standards would Rebekah's choice be considered wise or crazy? How does this example compare with the emphasis placed on finding the "right" person to marry in our society?
4. One criticism of marriage is that it is only a sexual relationship legalized by a piece of paper from the state. Discuss how the imagery of Ephesians 5:22-33 responds to that critique.
5. How can Christian women encourage their daughters in valuing the institution of marriage as stated in Hebrews 13:4 as well as assist them to develop their individual talents?

References

1. http://womenshistory.about.com/cs/quotes/a/ec_stanton.htm accessed January 26, 2015.
2. www.cdc.gov/std/stats/STI-Estimates-Fact-Sheet-February-2013.pdf accessed January 2015.
3. Smith, Helen, 2013. Men on Strike: Why Men are Boycotting Marriage, Fatherhood, and the American Dream-and Why it Matters. Encounter Books, New York, N.Y., United States.

CHAPTER FOUR

Source of Solutions (Part I): The Authority of God

Since Eve was faced with the choice to eat the fruit from the tree God had forbidden, every human being has faced the question, "Who will be in charge of my life?" In the first three chapters of this study, we exposed the satanic authority many of our countrymen and women have chosen to follow. If we would be the generation of Christian women to turn the tide in our country and the world against this evil, we must begin by recognizing God as our Supreme Authority and recognizing what it means for us to submit to Him. The Bible shows us examples of true and false obedience, some traps people get caught in that take them away from God, and how God would have us interact with people who choose not to follow the authority of God.

God created man and placed him in the Garden of Eden with only one direction:

> The LORD God commanded the man, saying, "From any tree of the garden you may eat freely; but from the tree of the knowledge of good and evil you shall not eat, for in the day that you eat from it you will surely die" (Genesis 2:16-17).

After the record of the creation of Eve, Genesis 3 begins with a conversation between Eve and the serpent. The Bible describes this serpent as "more crafty than any beast of the field which the Lord God had made" (Genesis 3:1). The reading continues.

53

> And he said to the woman, "Indeed, has God said, 'You shall not eat from any tree of the garden'?" The woman said to the serpent, "From the fruit of the trees of the garden we may eat; but from the fruit of the tree which is in the middle of the garden, God has said, 'You shall not eat from it or touch it, or you will die'" (Genesis 3:1-3).

The serpent was indeed crafty; he knew that Eve had been considering this one and only restriction to life in the Garden of Eden. He brought the subject up for discussion. Notice the perversion Eve has made to the direction by adding the words "or touch it." Satan takes advantage of her thoughts in his response to her.

> "You surely will not die! For God knows that in the day you eat from it your eyes will be opened, and you will be like God, knowing good and evil" (Genesis 3:4-5).

With these two thoughts, the serpent appealed to Eve's doubts about God's truthfulness and fairness. Would she really die? Was something important being kept from her by God? But most importantly, the serpent offered her the opportunity all humans seem to crave, the opportunity to be like God, to be her own authority, to be in charge of her own life. His words seemed so reasonable and surely to "know good and evil" had to be preferred over ignorance. Conspicuously absent from the serpent's smooth words was any description of consequences; in fact he deftly brushed them all aside with the three little letters, "not." Once Eve accepted his word that she would not die, she did not consider any other consequence.

> When the woman saw that the tree was good for food, and that it was a delight to the eyes, and that the tree was desirable to make one wise, she took from its fruit and ate; and she gave also to her husband with her, and he ate (Genesis 3:6).

Consequences immediately followed of course, and instead of joy, knowledge brought sorrow and the fracturing of the intimate friendship Adam and Eve enjoyed with God. As God responded to this sin, He directly addressed Eve's lust to be her own authority.

> To the woman He said, "I will greatly multiply your pain in childbirth, in pain will you bring forth children; yet your desire will be for your husband, and he will rule over you" (Genesis 3:16).

After Adam and Eve were expelled from the Garden, the account of humanity in the Old Testament is a continual repetition of the struggle between man and God for authority. As observers of these behaviors, we can discern some reasons for this disobedience so that we avoid these traps of Satan. In Genesis 4 we read the account of Cain and Abel.

> So it came about in the course of time that Cain brought an offering to the LORD of the fruit of the ground. Abel, on his part also brought of the firstlings of his flock and of their fat portions. And the LORD had regard for Abel and for his offering; but for Cain and for his offering He had no regard. So Cain became very angry and his countenance fell. Then the LORD said to Cain, "Why are you angry? And why has your countenance fallen? If you do well, will not your countenance be lifted up? And if you do not well, sin is crouching at the door; and its desire is for you, but you must master it" (Genesis 4:3-7).

As God spoke to Cain, He mentioned that Cain had not "done well" with regard to his sacrifice to the Lord. In Hebrews 11:4 Abel is commended as offering a better offering than Cain by faith. In Romans 10:17 we are told that faith comes by hearing the Word of God. It is reasonable for us to understand, therefore, that God did give directions to Cain and Abel for acceptable worship. Cain had decided not to accept God's authority on this but to offer what he *thought* was acceptable worship. This problem of man not worshiping according to God's plan continues today. In spite of their protestations that they are offering their love and glory to God, people continue to believe He will be pleased with worship given according to what pleases their senses. If we would live in faithful obedience to the authority of God we must resist the temptation of worship that stimulates our emotions

Source of Solutions (Part I): The Authority of God

and senses if it does not follow the pattern of worship laid down in God's Word.

Another example of this violation of God's authority in worship occurred with the children of Israel as they awaited Moses' return from communing with God on Mount Sinai. As Moses was receiving commands from God, the session was interrupted when God sent Moses back to the people.

> "Go down at once, for your people, whom you brought up from the land of Egypt, have corrupted themselves. They have quickly turned aside from the way which I commanded them. They have made for themselves a molten calf, and have worshiped it and have sacrificed to it and said, 'This is your god, O Israel, who brought you up from the land of Egypt!'" (Exodus 32:7-8)

Looking back to verse one of this chapter we see why this corruption occurred; the children of Israel got bored.

> Now when the people saw that Moses delayed to come down from the mountain, the people assembled about Aaron and said to him, "Come, make us a god who will go before us; as for this Moses, the man who brought us up from the land of Egypt, we do not know what has become of him" (Exodus 32:1).

Once again, man's changeable emotions and a short attention span were to blame for the people being unfaithful to God's authority. We are surrounded by a culture that values feelings and instant gratification in all things. In this atmosphere we are continually challenged to reject worship and spiritual philosophies that depend upon emotions and seek after the truth of God's authority, which stands the test of time and trials.

A pattern emerged after the children of Israel settled Canaan; the people of God would be blessed by Him, they would become comfortable in His prosperity, they would do what was right in their own eyes, God would punish them with wars, they would repent, and God would save them. The book of Judges recounts this pattern in detail. Eventually, the children of Israel begged Samuel for a king.

> Then all the elders of Israel gathered together and came to Samuel at Ramah; and they said to him, "Behold, you have grown old, and your sons do not walk in your ways. Now appoint a king for us to judge us like all the nations." But the thing was displeasing in the sight of Samuel when they said, "Give us a king to judge us." And Samuel prayed to the LORD. The LORD said to Samuel, "Listen to the voice of the people in regard to all that they say to you, for they have not rejected you, but they have rejected Me from being king over them. Like all the deeds which they have done since the day that I brought them up from Egypt even to this day—in that they have forsaken Me and served other gods—so they are doing to you also" (1 Samuel 8:4-8).

Samuel attempted to warn the people at the outset what their lives would be like with a king, but their response is worth consideration.

> Nevertheless, the people refused to listen to the voice of Samuel, and they said, "No, but there shall be a king over us, that we also may be like all the nations, that our king may judge us and go out before us and fight our battles" (1 Samuel 8:19-20).

The children of Israel wanted above all to be like all the other nations around them. They had taken on the values of the world around them and decided it was better to look like everyone else. They wanted a man to make their decisions and tell them what to do; they wanted to depend on that man to fight their battles for them. Having the advantage of the Bible to inform us how this decision worked out for them, it is easy to chide them for turning away from God; the question for us to consider is how often do we make the same choice? Given one of the reasons the elders gave to Samuel for having a king was that his sons were not faithful to God, is it possible these elders believed having a good king like the other nations would not be turning away from God's authority at all? Do we make choices about our lives, deciding that "good" people outside the church are better to associate with than the men we perceive as hypocritical or old-fashioned leaders in our congregations?

From the account of the disobedience of Achan in Joshua 7 and the punishment the children of Israel received as a result, we know that while God led the children of Israel He insisted on their obedience to His directions.

> Joshua said, "Alas O Lord GOD, why did you ever bring this people over the Jordan, only to deliver us into the hand of the Amorites, to destroy us? If only we had been willing to dwell beyond the Jordan! O Lord, what can I say since Israel has turned their back before their enemies? For the Canaanites and all the inhabitants of the land will hear of it, and they will surround us and cut off our name from the earth. And what will You do for Your great name?" So the LORD said to Joshua, "Rise up! Why is it that you have fallen on your face? Israel has sinned, and they have also transgressed My covenant which I commanded them. And they have even taken some of the things under the ban and have both stolen and deceived. Moreover, they have also put them among their own things. Therefore the sons of Israel cannot stand before their enemies; they turn their backs before their enemies, for they have become accursed. I will not be with you anymore unless you destroy the things under the ban from your midst" (Joshua 7:7-12).

As quoted in the passage from 1 Samuel 8, a king would judge and go to battle for the people, but the children of Israel did not expect their king to insist on moral obedience. They wanted a secular ruler. They wanted to look like the nations around them; one aspect was they wanted religion and government to be separate. So God said, "...they have rejected Me from being king over them" (1 Samuel 8:7).

Looking into the New Testament, we see how hundreds of years of secular rule had completed the apostasy of the children of God from His authority. Jesus was born into a nation of Israel held captive by the Roman Empire. Religious observances and politics overshadowed the faith of God's chosen people. The authority of God had been replaced by the Sanhedrin and the contentious sects of the Pharisees and Sadducees. Jesus' teachings were uncomfortable to the Jewish elite because He called the multitudes back to the authority of God. The gospel of John details some of the verbal confrontations the Jews had with Jesus as their fear of His teaching and His miracles grew. After Jesus raised Lazarus from the dead the religious rulers met together and said,

> "...What are we doing? For this man is performing many signs. If we let Him go on like this, all men will believe in Him, and the Romans will come and take away both our place and our nation" (John 11:47-48).

God gave Peter, James, and John confirmation of Jesus' supremacy over Moses and Elijah during a special encounter on a mountain.

> Some eight days after these sayings, He took along Peter and John and James, and went up on the mountain to pray. And while He was praying, the appearance of His face became different, and His clothing became white and gleaming. And behold, two men were talking with Him; and they were Moses and Elijah, who, appearing in glory, were speaking of His departure which He was about to accomplish at Jerusalem... And as these were leaving Him, Peter said to Jesus, "Master, it is good for us to be here; let us make three tabernacles: one for You, and one for Moses, and one for Elijah"—not realizing what he was saying. While he was saying this, a cloud formed and began to overshadow them; and they were afraid as they entered the cloud. Then a voice came out of the cloud, saying, "This is My Son, My Chosen One; listen to Him!" And when the voice had spoken, Jesus was found alone (Luke 9:28-31, 33-36).

As Jesus prepared to sacrifice Himself, He offered a prayer to His Father. In this prayer as recorded in John's Gospel, Jesus said,

> "Father, the hour has come; glorify Your Son, that the Son may glorify You, even as You gave Him authority over all flesh, that to all whom You have given Him, He may give eternal life" (John 17:1-2).

As Jesus stood in front of Pilate before being crucified, we read the following conversation.

Source of Solutions (Part I): The Authority of God

> "Are You the King of the Jews?"...Jesus answered, "My kingdom is not of this world. If My kingdom were of this world, then My servants would be fighting so that I would not be handed over to the Jews; but as it is, My kingdom is not of this realm." Therefore Pilate said to Him, "So You are a king?" Jesus answered, "You say correctly that I am a king. For this I have been born, and for this I have come into the world, to testify to the truth. Everyone who is of the truth hears My voice" (John 18:33-37).

At the end of the Gospel of Matthew, in the passage commonly referred to by Christians as the "Great Commission," Jesus says of Himself, "All authority has been given to Me in heaven and on earth" (Matthew 28:18).

Paul wrote about the authority of Jesus in the letter to the Christians at Colossae.

> He is the image of the invisible God, the firstborn of all creation. For by Him all things were created, both in the heavens and on earth, visible and invisible, whether thrones or dominions or rulers or authorities—all things have been created through Him and for Him. He is before all things, and in Him all things hold together. He is also head of the body, the church; and He is the beginning, the firstborn from the dead, so that He Himself will come to have first place in everything (Colossians 1:15-18).

Paul exhorted Christians in his epistles not to be distracted from focusing on Christ as their authority. After rebuking the Corinthian church for dividing their loyalties among Christ, the brother Apollo, and the apostle Peter, he reminded them of the bedrock of the gospel.

> For indeed Jews ask for signs and Greeks search for wisdom; but we preach Christ crucified, to Jews a stumbling block and to Gentiles foolishness, but to those who are the called, both Jews and Greeks, Christ the power of God and the wisdom of God (1 Corinthians 1:22-24).

Today in denominations, as well as in the church, people succumb to the temptation to follow men and women who appeal to their hearts, rather than follow Jesus. Any church that holds up a preacher or teacher, is divided into clergy and laity, or follows a pope or a prophet's leadership is not following the authority of Jesus as the only Head of the church.

In the letter of Paul to the Galatians, he denounced those who would distract the brethren from the supreme authority of Christ.

> "I am amazed that you are so quickly deserting Him who called you by the grace of Christ, for a different gospel; which is really not another; only there are some who are disturbing you and want to distort the gospel of Christ. But even if we, or an angel from heaven, should preach to you a gospel contrary to what we have preached to you, he is to be accursed! As we have said before, so I say again now, if any man is preaching to you a gospel contrary to what you received, he is to be accursed! For am I now seeking the favor of men, or of God? Or am I striving to please men? If I were still trying to please men, I would not be a bond-servant of Christ" (Galatians 1:6-10).

This passage implies that just as it was from the time of Eve, the doctrine leading the new Christians away from the truth of the Gospel was pleasing to the senses of the hearers. It was more pleasing than the teaching of Christ. Paul condemned the false teachers without restraint. He expressed confidence that any teaching different from the truth already taught to the Galatian Christians would be false.

Paul warned the elders of the church at Ephesus during his last meeting with them about false teachers, saying,

> Be on guard for yourselves and for all the flock, among which the Holy Spirit has made you overseers, to shepherd the church of God which He purchased with His own blood. I know that after my departure savage wolves will come in among you, not sparing the flock; and from among your own selves men will arise, speaking perverse things, to draw away the disciples after them (Acts 20:28-30).

Paul was not the only New Testament author to warn the first-century Christians against false teaching. The writer of the book of Hebrews also had stern warnings.

> Anyone who has set aside the Law of Moses dies without mercy on the testimony of two or three witnesses. How much severer punishment do you think he will deserve who has trampled under foot the Son of God, and has regarded as unclean the blood of the covenant by which he was sanctified, and has insulted the Spirit of grace? (Hebrews 10:28-29)

Peter also warned the Christians,

> As obedient children, do not be conformed to the former lusts which were yours in your ignorance, but like the Holy One who called you, be holy yourselves also in all your behavior (1 Peter 1:14-15).

The apostle John discussed at length in his epistles how Christians can be confident that they are walking in Christ.

> By this we know that we have come to know Him, if we keep His commandments. The one who says, "I have come to know Him," and does not keep His commandments, is a liar, and the truth is not in him; but whoever keeps His word, in him the love of God has truly been perfected. By this we know that we are in Him: the one who says he abides in Him ought himself to walk in the same manner as He walked (1 John 2:3-6).

The apostle known for his writings on love did not shrink from calling false teachers liars.

> For many deceivers have gone out into the world, those who do not acknowledge Jesus Christ as coming in the flesh. This is the deceiver and the antichrist. Watch yourselves, that you do not lose what we have accomplished, but that you may receive a full reward. Anyone who goes too far and does not abide in the teaching of Christ, does not have God; the one who abides in the teaching, he has both the Father and the Son. If anyone comes to you and does not bring this teaching, do not receive him into your house, and do not give him a greeting; for the one who gives him a greeting participates in his evil deeds (2 John 1:7-11).

This passage is not a popular one in our age of tolerance, ecumenicalism, and political correctness. If we would abide by the authority of Jesus and teach the whole truth, we must begin to live this teaching. We have seen in this review of the human response to the authority of God in the Scriptures that it is more common for humans to disobey God than to obey Him. We have seen that Satan knows our doubts about God's commands and that he knows how to manipulate our doubts and emotions to get us to accept falsehood. We have seen that false teaching is, as a rule, easier to follow than the truth because it is more widely accepted. Often the reason for that wide acceptance is that false teaching does not demand any change in our hearts, our thought processes, or our behaviors, and it stimulates our emotions in pleasing ways.

In the verses quoted above the inspired apostle John tells us that we are not to give assistance to the teachers of religious error. In other words, we are not to assist their ministries or wish them success on them. Is this discrimination? Our secular society has conditioned us to believe that all discrimination is wrong. However, this Scripture does not teach us to treat these erring people badly; it teaches us not to support their false teaching. Instead we ought to be trying to teach them the truth. This is a form of discrimination I believe Christians need to practice with firm resolve. Jesus warned,

> "Not everyone who says to Me, 'Lord, Lord,' will enter the kingdom of heaven, but he who does the will of My Father who is in heaven will enter. Many will say to me on that day, 'Lord, Lord, did we not prophesy in Your name, and in Your name cast out demons, and in Your name perform many miracles?' And then I will declare to them, 'I never knew you; DEPART FROM ME, YOU WHO PRACTICE LAWLESSNESS'" (Matthew 7:21-23).

The decision to become a Christian by being immersed in water for the forgiveness of our sins according to Scriptures such as Acts 2:38 is the first of countless decisions we make about our obedience to Christ. Satan is always at our side with the easy, pleasing way to disobey the authority of Christ. The apostles of Christ went to their deaths defending the place of Christ as Supreme Authority over the religious teachings of man. The inspired writers of the Bible left us with the ability to know with confidence what God's will is for us. It is our responsibility to study and put into practice God's will faithfully and courageously and joyfully, basing our practice on truth rather than human reasoning; persevering rather than giving in to the latest trend; keeping focused on Jesus rather than becoming disciples of the latest smooth-talking teacher or singer; and being the example for others of steadfast, hopeful faithfulness to the authority of Jesus.

CHAPTER FOUR **Questions for Discussion**

1. We make thousands of choices every day. How important is the choice to accept the authority of God? How often do we make that choice?

2. Discuss positive ways our choice to be obedient to God's authority can affect our relationships in our workplace and in our community.

3. Usually it is easier to accept the authority of human figures, such as teachers or doctors, once we have respect and trust for them. Reflect and share with the class some ways God has earned your respect and trust.

4. The apostles, Paul, Peter, and John, all spoke plainly of those who taught false doctrine. Considering their directness in dealing with this issue, how can Christian women today guard against being led away from the truth of the Bible?

CHAPTER FIVE

Source of Solutions (Part 2): Valuing Human Life

Without a doubt, the most disturbing experience of my recent pursuit of an advanced nursing degree came during a management class. To improve nurses' abilities to manage other personnel we had to study different philosophies of life. In my reading for the class, I learned that the philosophy of feminism was the "situation ethics" of the 1960s dressed up in new clothes. Feminists do whatever the situation calls for to advance their agenda; if they get the job done, then what they have done is right. Utilitarianism and feminism and pragmatism were all presented in my textbook as being far superior to any system of ethics or morality, especially religious systems.

This was disturbing enough, but I had determined just to get through the class. The PowerPoint presentations dragged on, rehashing the information I had read. Eventually the professor began her lecture. She was determined to drive home the points of the book by taking them farther. I pricked up my ears when she began talking about the fact that there were no moral absolutes. A young male student behind me tentatively spoke up and said that he believed in the "Golden Rule." The professor took an authoritative physical stance and stated, "I don't believe in 'Do unto others as you would have them do unto you;' I believe in doing unto others as they want to be done by. I do not believe in absolutes."

At this point, for the sake of all the young people in my class—I should point out that I was old enough to be the mother of 90 percent of the class—I confronted the professor. "I do believe in the absolute value of every human life," I said.

I was sitting in the front row of the class, and suddenly this became an uncomfortable seat. The professor closed the distance between us, looked down on me, and gave me a "What if?" scenario designed to weaken my resolve. "Suppose you are working on a hospital floor and are assigned to care for a man who is a convicted serial killer? What would you do?"

I don't know what she expected me to say, perhaps that I would hide in the linen closet or something. She was not prepared for my response: "I would remember that as a nurse it was not my place to punish this man, and it was not required that I like him. It was my job to take care of his physical problems as I had been ordered to do in a professional and compassionate manner because he was a human being. I would trust the justice system to take care of his crimes. I would utilize my other team members to vent about my discomfort appropriately, and when I got off work, I would take steps to relieve my stress so it did not build up and cause burn out."

The professor's jaw dropped. She sputtered for a second and then gasped out, "Do you know what a high standard that is?" She was not complimenting me. I ruined her image of the self-righteous person who believed in absolutes. She was frustrated and ended the lecture as quickly as she could. She did not speak to me again that day. I left the class session hoping our exchange would cause the other students to doubt the philosophical nonsense they had been fed in that class session.

It should be significant to readers of this account this occurred in a nursing class full of new RNs. Young nurses are being taught that compassionate care for the people to whom they are assigned may not be as important as other factors, such as efficiency.

Nursing has long had a reputation as the most trusted profession in our country. That stunning class session, where I had to take a stand for the value of human life, is the motivation for this study. As catalysts for the return to Christianity, one area in which women need to speak out is in defense of the value of human life.

When the subject of human life is introduced today, most people assume a discussion of abortion is going to follow. Certainly the epidemic of abortions in the United States since the Supreme Court legalized the procedure in 1973 is one of the blackest moral blemishes on this country. More than 53 million babies have been murdered in the United States between the passage of Roe vs. Wade and 2011, according to a report published online by the Guttmacher Institute in July 2014.[1] In our study, though, we will look at how Jesus taught and lived the principle of valuing human life with people of all ages. Concern for the souls of those with whom we share this planet ought to be a top priority to us, so we will learn from Jesus' example.

As Christians, we take for granted that Jesus values us because of His sacrifice for our souls. Having repeatedly read and heard lessons on the Great Commission of Matthew 28, we know we are to love souls and try to teach the gospel to all mankind. But when our gospel meetings and Vacation Bible Schools draw fewer of our own church members, much less people from the community, and our door-knocking campaigns and flyer mailings have no results, we are left with the question, "How do we reach people today?" We live our daily lives attending church activities, struggling with road rage during our commutes, hearing about cyber-bullying that results in junior high girls and boys committing suicide, purchasing home security systems in the hope of preventing home invasions holding our breath every time another shooting is announced on the news, and wondering how it could happen again. We move to the other side of the street to avoid walking past the group of tattooed young people and thank God our kids are not outrageous like that; we swallow our disgust at the effeminate behavior of the flamboyantly dressed male at the hair salon; we see a woman wearing a *hijab*-shaped headscarf walking down the street and feel anger because of the behavior of others who profess that religion. I believe it is prudent for us to take precautions to protect ourselves against wanton violence. I also believe it is difficult for the dangers mentioned above not to erode our ability to value human life. We can benefit from being reminded of the examples and teachings of Jesus regarding the value of the people of this world. As we begin to value purposefully the people around us, we may open doors for the gospel as Jesus did.

Jesus was never too busy to spend time with children. The Scripture bears out that He found their sincerity, honesty, and innocence a refreshing change from the political posturing of even His disciples.

> At that time the disciples came to Jesus and said, "Who then is the greatest in the kingdom of heaven?" And He called a child to Himself and set him before them, and said, "Truly I say to you, unless you are converted and become like children, you will not enter the kingdom of heaven. Whoever then humbles himself as this child, he is the greatest in the kingdom of heaven. And whoever receives one such child in My name receives Me; but whoever causes one of these little ones who believe in Me to stumble, it would be better for him to have a heavy millstone hung around his neck, and to be drowned in the depth of the sea" (Matthew 18:1-6).

Luke records another occasion where Jesus showed His love for children.

> And they were bringing even their babies to Him so that He would touch them, but when the disciples saw it, they began rebuking them. But Jesus called for them, saying, "Permit the children to come to Me, and do not hinder them, for the kingdom of God belongs to such as these. Truly I say to you, whoever

does not receive the kingdom of God like a child will not enter it at all" (Luke 18:15-17).

In John 4 there is a long account of Jesus' conversation with a Samaritan woman. There were a number of reasons Jesus was not supposed to be talking to this woman. She was a woman alone and casual conversation between the sexes was not socially acceptable in that culture. She was a Samaritan, and in verse 9 we read, "For Jews have no dealings with Samaritans." She was immoral, and Jesus knew her history because of His omniscience. In verse 18 He confronted her with this truth. But Jesus saw in this woman a soul, and He valued her enough to breach all of these conventions to have a conversation with her. In the rest of verse 9 of this chapter, we read that this woman did not respond positively to Jesus' first overture to her: "Therefore the Samaritan woman said to Him, 'How is it that You, being a Jew, ask me for a drink since I am a Samaritan woman?'" (John 4:9) Throughout the conversation, the woman's responses indicated distrust in Jesus and prejudice against the Jews. Jesus was not put off that she was not overwhelmed with gratitude that He would speak to her. He calmly instructed her in the truth. His persistence and respectful conversation along with His prior knowledge of her life eventually won over her prejudice and skepticism.

Sometimes after much inner struggle, we courageously reach out to someone who we consider socially undesirable because we know we should. Maybe we volunteer at a homeless shelter or a women's shelter. If the people we are trying to help respond with distrust or prejudice against us, do we give up in anger that they didn't recognize the favor we were doing for them? Or do we offer them respect and kindness, giving them a reason to trust us? In caring for new patients, I have learned just because I know I have skill and the best of motivations does not mean a person who has lost her independence and health is going to believe it. It is through offering kindness, respect, and listening rather than talking, that I earn respect and trust. This applies to people in the spiritual sphere as well. Working with people takes time, and they are more likely to listen to us after we have listened to them and treated them with dignity. Smiling, speaking someone's name, looking them in the eye and offering sincere gladness to meet them are all good ways to express to someone that we value them.

In Matthew 15 there is an interesting account of Jesus' interaction with another woman.

> And a Canaanite woman from that region came out and began to cry out, saying, "Have mercy on me, Lord, Son of David; my daughter is cruelly demon-possessed." But He did not answer her a word. And His disciples came and implored Him, saying, "Send her away, because she keeps shouting at us." But He answered and said, "I was sent only to the lost sheep of the house of Israel." But she came and began to bow down before Him, saying, "Lord, help me!" And He answered and said, "It is not good to take the children's bread and throw it to the dogs." But she said, "Yes, Lord; but even the dogs feed on the crumbs which fall from their masters' table." Then Jesus said to her, "O woman, your faith is great; it shall be done for you as you wish." And her daughter was healed at once (Matthew 15:22-28).

The first glance at this passage might give the impression that Jesus was exhibiting prejudice toward this woman because she was not a Jew. However, the key to Jesus' purpose was made clear in His final response to her. By her persistence in continuing to cry out to Jesus and replying to His figure of speech in kind, she exhibited her faith in Jesus, showing she was not just following rumors she might have heard about His power. He valued her as a person and also her choice to believe in Him.

Throughout Jesus' ministry, He had repeated conflicts with the Pharisees and Sadducees, those who the masses of Jews had been conditioned to believe were the most righteous of their people. He continually showed by His teaching and behavior that He valued the sinners of society. Toward the beginning of Jesus' ministry, as He was gathering His disciples, He found a tax collector.

> As Jesus went on from there, He saw a man called Matthew, sitting in the tax collector's booth; and He said to him, "Follow Me!" And he got up and followed Him. Then it happened that as Jesus was reclining at the table in the house, behold, many tax collectors and sinners came and were dining with Jesus and His disciples. When the Pharisees saw this, they said to His disciples, "Why is your Teacher eating with the tax collectors and sinners?" But when Jesus heard this, He said, "It is not those who are healthy who need a physician, but those who are sick. But go and learn what this means: 'I DESIRE COMPASSION, AND NOT SACRIFICE,' for I did not come to call the righteous, but sinners" (Matthew 9:9-13).

Jesus did not come to earth to associate with those who already considered themselves morally sufficient. He wanted to be with those who knew they needed help. He explains this clearly in Luke 18.

> "Two men went up into the temple to pray, one a Pharisee and the other a tax collector. The Pharisee stood and was praying this to himself: 'God, I thank You that I am not like other people: swindlers, unjust, adulterers, or even like this tax collector. I fast twice a week; I pay tithes of all that I get.' "But the tax collector, standing some distance away, was even unwilling to lift up his eyes to heaven, but was beating his breast, saying, 'God be merciful to me, the sinner!' I tell you, this man went to his house justified rather than the other; for everyone who exalts himself will be humbled, but he who humbles himself will be exalted" (Luke 18:10-14).

It is important as we consider Jesus' example of valuing sinners to understand His goal in working with them was to bring them to repentance. The next two passages illustrate this. Jesus found another tax collector, Zaccheus.

> And there was a man called by the name of Zaccheus; he was a chief tax collector and he was rich. Zaccheus was trying to see

Source of Solutions (Part 2): Valuing Human Life

who Jesus was, and was unable because of the crowd, for he was small in stature. So he ran on ahead and climbed up into a sycamore tree in order to see Him, for He was about to pass through that way. When Jesus came to the place, He looked up and said to him, "Zaccheus, hurry and come down, for today I must stay at your house." And he hurried and came down and received Him gladly. When they saw it, they all began to grumble, saying, "He has gone to be the guest of a man who is a sinner." Zaccheus stopped and said to the Lord, "Behold, Lord, half of my possessions I will give to the poor, and if I have defrauded anyone of anything, I will give back four times as much." And Jesus said to him, "Today salvation has come to this house, because he, too, is a son of Abraham" (Luke 19:2-9).

Tax collectors were considered collaborators with the Romans who oppressed the Jews. Everyone despised them, even more so than we despise the IRS today! Jesus did not have to compromise Himself in associating with Zaccheus, but He valued him as a precious soul in need of salvation. Jesus had the advantage of knowing all hearts, even knowing that Zaccheus would be open to Him.

In John 8 there is a dramatic illustration of the priority Jesus placed on winning the individual soul.

> The scribes and the Pharisees brought a woman caught in adultery, and having set her in the center of the court, they said to Him, "Teacher, this woman has been caught in adultery, in the very act. Now in the Law Moses commanded us to stone such women; what then do You say?" They were saying this, testing Him, so that they might have grounds for accusing Him. But Jesus stooped down and with His finger wrote on the ground. But when they persisted in asking Him, He straightened up, and said to them, "He who is without sin among you, let him be the first to throw a stone at her." Again He stooped down and wrote on the ground. When they heard it, they began to go out one by one, beginning with the older ones, and He was left alone, and the woman, where she was, in the center of the court. Straightening up, Jesus said to her, "Woman, where are

they? Did no one condemn you?" She said, "No one, Lord." And Jesus said. "I do not condemn you either. Go. From now on sin no more" (John 8:3-11).

Jesus was aware of the Pharisees unjust usage of this woman to test Him. He did not engage in their game. He did not condemn her according to the Mosaic Law. However, He did not give approval to the behavior in which He knew she had been engaged. He told her not to do it again. It is my own speculation, but I would guess this experience and conversation with Jesus was a powerful motivator to the woman to change her behavior.

Even Jesus did not win over every sinner. A tragic passage in Matthew 23 illustrates that he valued the disobedient even though they would incur punishment for their rebellion.

> "Jerusalem, Jerusalem, who kills the prophets and stones those who are sent to her! How often I wanted to gather your children together, the way a hen gathers her chicks under her wings, and you were unwilling. Behold, your house is being left to you desolate!" (Matthew 23:37-38)

Even Jesus' authority did not allow Him to accept those sinners who refused to repent. This is an important principle we would do well to remember as we deal with those who choose to rebel against the teachings of the gospel.

Jesus also valued the elderly. As it has sadly begun to happen in our day, there were those in Jesus' day who did not honor the elderly.

> Then some Pharisees and scribes came to Jesus from Jerusalem and said, "Why do Your disciples break the tradition of the elders? For they do not wash their hands when they eat bread." And He answered and said to them, "Why do you yourselves transgress the commandment of God for the sake of your tradition? For God said, 'HONOR YOUR FATHER AND MOTHER' and 'HE WHO SPEAKS EVIL OF FATHER OR MOTHER IS TO BE PUT TO DEATH.' But you say, 'Whoever says to his father or mother, "Whatever I have that would help you has been given to God" he is not to

honor his father or his mother.' And by this you have invalidated the word of God for the sake of your tradition. You hypocrites, rightly did Isaiah prophesy of you, 'THIS PEOPLE HONORS ME WITH THEIR LIPS, BUT THEIR HEART IS FAR AWAY FROM ME. BUT IN VAIN DO THEY WORSHIP ME, TEACHING AS DOCTRINES THE PRECEPTS OF MEN'" (Matthew 15:1-9).

As Jesus neared the end of His life in agony and humiliation, His last thoughts included His own mother. John records the following:

> But standing by the cross of Jesus were His mother, and His mother's sister, Mary the wife of Clopas, and Mary Magdalene. When Jesus then saw His mother, and the disciple whom He loved standing nearby, He said to His mother, "Woman, behold your son!" Then He said to the disciple, "Behold, your mother!" From that hour the disciple took her into his own household (John 19:25b-27).

Jesus had much to do during the three years of His ministry, but He always had time for individuals. His purpose was to value and lift up the forgotten, unimportant people. From the poor, the children, the races thought to be unclean by the religious elite, to sinners, enemies, and the elderly, He valued them all. And we rejoice that He did, for in honest reflection, we know we all fit into some of those categories sometimes in our lives!

As we contemplate being courageous servants of Christ, we cannot ignore these precedents from His life. It is difficult to get out of our suburban routines to find those lost along the way. It would be so much easier if our neighbors in the community, the ones with the well-behaved kids and the beautiful yards, would be willing to study with us. We need to attempt to interest them because their souls are valuable to God, but most of the time, they are comfortable in their morality, their religion, their routine. The people we are more likely to reach are the ones whose lives have been interrupted or destroyed by sin, disease, or some other disaster. Sometimes these can be as close as the people we work with but do not really know. Others may be farther away from our lives, but they are still in need: the ones who fight addiction and know they cannot do it on their own; the people whose decisions in youth have left them with broken relationships, poverty, and children to raise on their own; or the women who exercised their "choice" and now live with the shame and pain from what was supposed to be a painless procedure to eradicate lifeless tissue. We cannot bring back the lives of the aborted babies by protesting abortion clinics. We can bring these women hope for new joy and life in Christ, free from the shame of the past.

Almost daily we have more reason to sorrow over the decay of our culture: more murders, more suicides, more abandonments, new illicit drugs, more families and more lives torn apart. If we would see a return to God in our culture, if we would see societal repentance for national sins, then the uncomfortable answer lies with us. We must find ways to leave our comfortable subdivisions and venture to the places where men, women, and children wander in need of basic necessities, as well as the knowledge of God. Some Christians may be able to look in the eyes of the addict and the alcoholic and listen to their stories and offer them hope. Some may be able to foster or adopt babies and children who otherwise would have no home. Some may be able to assist the home-bound elderly men and women who have no one else to care for them. Some may be able to reach to women or young people in the prison system. If more Christians entered the prisons with the truth of the gospel, I wonder if there would be as many radicalized Muslims coming out of them.

We all have different talents. Each of us can relate to different types of people. The single women in our congregations have the freedom and time to reach out to more people than the married women. Those with families need to balance the responsibilities of their homes and families with reaching out to others, since our children are our first evangelistic responsibility and our husbands our highest commitment except God. However, the kinds of service and evangelism I am discussing cannot be accomplished by making our churches into soup kitchens; programs are not what people need. The New Testament does not teach by command, example, or inference that the church is to take on this kind of service as a group. The down-trodden, socially unacceptable people need individual Christians to befriend them, gain their trust, and show them the sincere service that comes from following the example of Jesus.

Following these radical suggestions requires much of us emotionally and physically. It requires a change in our priorities from comfort to service. Our love for Jesus and desire to show gratitude by obeying Him are a great place to start in developing love for others. If we pray for His direction and opportunities to reach out to others, would He fail to provide them? Some training or education may be needed in working with people whose life experiences are so different from our own. Volunteering in shelters, hospitals, assisted living facilities, or nursing homes can be a good way to learn in a controlled and safe setting. We must use wisdom in choosing areas in which to serve that will not put us or the children we bring with us in danger and will not support false doctrine. But there are many types of places suitable for even the person most inexperienced in serving. Persistence in searching for the right place will be rewarded.

Every relationship we develop in those settings is another opportunity to share with others the hope of salvation through Christ. As we engage in serving the sea of humanity around us, we remember not everyone will come to Christ; we recognize each person's right of choice just as Jesus did. We move on in love for others so everyone may have opportunity to learn the truth, we do so because we value all human life.

CHAPTER FIVE **Questions for Discussion**

1. Do you relate more easily to younger people or older people?
2. Have you ever volunteered in your community? Share one learning experience you had in that effort.
3. Are you aware of volunteering opportunities in your community working with children, teenagers, adults, or the elderly? Discuss existing opportunities with your class.
4. If you are unable to go out to volunteer yourself, would you be willing to support others who go out by babysitting children or providing meals for their family?
5. How could volunteering in a group with community members outside the church open additional doors for the gospel where you live?
6. If you are single, have you ever considered getting involved in disaster relief in your own country or overseas? Have you ever gone on a mission trip?
7. How does choosing to value the souls of the people with whom you interact help your attitude toward service?

Reference

1. http://www.guttmacher.org/pubs/fb_induced_abortion.html Fact Sheet: Abortion in the United States, accessed January 17, 2015.

CHAPTER SIX

Finding Courage (Part 1): Our Weakness, God's Strength

When we read passages like Hebrews 11 about the faithful people of the Old Testament who endured so much hardship, we are left with a sense of wonder at their dedication. When we read through the book of Acts about the persecutions faced by the Christians of the early church, we are left with awe and admiration for what they suffered for their faith. When we look in our mirrors, though, we see our imperfections: physical, spiritual, and otherwise. We see ordinary women with fears and weaknesses we struggle against daily. Maybe we see reflections of scars of past mistreatment, sorrows that haunt our footsteps decades after events in our personal histories, or consequences of choices of our own or other people. These issues we can't get past make us feel less than useful to God in our own eyes.

With such a perspective already at work in our minds, reading the material in the first chapters of this book regarding the great need in the world can be more than discouraging. The material can be difficult to believe and overwhelming to consider. It is one thing to read about Mordecai telling Esther she may have been born for "such a time as this." We cannot conceive this could be true for ourselves, given what we know about our own flaws and mistakes. Considering the demands of our lives, it may seem that much of the time we are doing well to get from one Sunday service to the next without some kind of crisis. When we are barely

Finding Courage (Part 1): Our Weakness, God's Strength

hanging on ourselves, how can we think of a larger purpose?

In this study let us consider courage in the lives of a few heroes of faith from the Old and New Testaments. What is courage? Where does it come from? How is it kept alive? What is the purpose of having courage?

In Exodus 2 we read about the birth of Moses. In his life there is much to consider about the quality of courage.

> Now it came about in those days, when Moses had grown up, that he went out to his brethren and looked on their hard labors; and he saw an Egyptian beating a Hebrew, one of his brethren. So he looked this way and that, and when he saw there was no one around, he struck down the Egyptian and hid him in the sand. He went out the next day, and behold, two Hebrews were fighting with each other; and he said to the offender, "Why are your striking your companion?" But he said, "Who made you a prince or a judge over us? Are you intending to kill me as you killed the Egyptian?" Then Moses was afraid and said, "Surely the matter has become known." When Pharaoh heard of this matter, he tried to kill Moses. But Moses fled from the presence of Pharaoh and settled in the land of Midian, and he sat down by a well (Exodus 2:11-15).

We can see in this passage that Moses had a worldly courage. It was based on his pride in himself and his own strength. He was outraged by the plight of his people and perceived he was in the perfect position to liberate them. He did not seek out God's plan but moved on his own in this defense of one of them. His action did not have the result he anticipated, and he had to run away to Midian. Moses went from being a prince in Egypt as Pharaoh's daughter's son to being a murderer. He lost his fame and became a humble shepherd in a foreign land.

Many years later, God came to call Moses to liberate the Hebrews from Egypt. From the burning bush on the side of Mt. Horeb, God revealed His plan.

> He said also, "I am the God of your father, the God of Abraham,

the God of Isaac, and the God of Jacob." Then Moses hid his face, for he was afraid to look at God... "Now, behold, the cry of the sons of Israel has come to me; furthermore, I have seen the oppression with which the Egyptians are oppressing them. Therefore, come now, and I will send you to Pharaoh, so that you may bring My people, the sons of Israel, out of Egypt." But Moses said to God, "Who am I, that I should go to Pharaoh, and that I should bring the sons of Israel out of Egypt?" (Exodus 3:6, 9-11)

Moses' response to God's declaration manifested the humility he learned from his mistaken attempt to liberate his people years ago. His thinking regarding his fitness for the mission of liberating the sons of Israel had gone from one extreme to the other—from believing he was the best person to believing he was not suited for it at all. In one sense Moses was correct. The only qualification he possessed to do this great work was God had called Him to do so. Through the rest of chapter 3 and into chapter 4 Moses conversed with God, trying to convince God He had chosen the wrong leader. God had an answer for each of Moses' objections, and they give us insight into elements of godly courage that can help us.

In addition to questioning his own fitness for this task, Moses wanted to know how he would convince the Hebrews that he was a credible leader. God responded by giving Moses the best credential he could have—the command from the eternal God, the God of Abraham, Isaac, and Jacob. Moses then wanted to know how he would ever convince Pharaoh to let God's people go. God informed Moses His plan was not just to free the Hebrews from slavery; God's plan was also to show His own power and authority over Pharaoh and the false gods of Egypt. So God told Moses that Pharaoh would not let the children of Israel go to worship Him easily. He gave Moses the ability to perform limited signs to convince Pharaoh of his authenticity as leader of Israel. As Moses continued to resist God's command, insisting he was not a good speaker, God allowed Moses' brother, Aaron, to speak as his mouthpiece. God gave Moses everything he needed to obey the command to lead His people. For Moses to act with Godly courage was to obey this command and to save lives by challenging the unjust rule of the Pharaoh. The details of this commission are found in Exodus 3:10-4:19.

Through the process of working with Pharaoh to free the sons of Israel, Moses had to combat his fears.

> Now the LORD spoke to Moses, saying, "Go, tell Pharaoh king of Egypt to let the sons of Israel go out of his land." But Moses spoke before the LORD, saying, "Behold, the sons of Israel have not listened to me; how then will Pharaoh listen to me, for I am unskilled in speech?" (Exodus 6:10-12)

This complaint from Moses is repeated in verse 30 of this chapter. As Moses focused on himself and his own ability, he was unable to carry out his mission to speak to Pharaoh. God had to remind him repeatedly He was the One in conflict with Pharaoh, and He would be the One bringing the children of Israel to freedom.

> "When Pharaoh does not listen to you, then I will lay My hand on Egypt and bring out My hosts, My people the sons of Israel, from the land of Egypt by great judgments." (Exodus 7:4)

As Moses witnessed God's powerful interactions with Pharaoh, he came to understand his place as messenger. By the time the sons of Israel came out from Egypt to camp near the Red Sea, there was no doubt in his mind any longer about God's power to work through him to lead His people. Notice the transformation in his heart and the conviction with which he spoke to the fearful Hebrews in the following exchange:

> Then they said to Moses, "Is it because there were no graves in Egypt that you have taken us away to die in the wilderness? Why have you dealt with us in this way, bringing us out of Egypt? Is this not the word that we spoke to you in Egypt, saying 'Leave us alone that we may serve the Egyptians'? For it would have

been better for us to serve the Egyptians than to die in the wilderness." But Moses said to the people, "Do not fear! Stand by and see the salvation of the LORD which He will accomplish for you today; for the Egyptians whom you have seen today, you will never see them again forever. The LORD will fight for you while you keep silent" (Exodus 14:11-14).

Notice, this passage recorded Moses uttered these words to the sons of Israel himself, not through Aaron, the mouthpiece God had appointed. The words of Moses in this passage were a magnificent declaration of the godly courage in his heart as leader of the sons of Israel. He had stepped completely outside himself and his fears. At that moment, he was allowing God to do more with him than he believed he could do. His complete trust in God's power had freed him from his fear of his own inadequacies and from his memory of his past sins. And as long as Moses continued in this mindset of obedient faith in God, he experienced freedom from his past and his shortcomings.

We know he lost this mindset one tragic time as he led the sons of Israel through the desert for forty years. He forgot his place as the vessel through which God was working to lead His people to the land He had promised them.

> So Moses took the rod from before the LORD, just as He had commanded him; and Moses and Aaron gathered the assembly before the rock. And he said to them, "Listen now, you rebels; shall we bring forth water for you out of this rock?" Then Moses lifted up his hand and struck the rock twice with his rod; and water came forth abundantly, and the congregation and their beasts drank. But the LORD said to Moses and Aaron, "Because you have not believed Me, to treat Me as holy in the sight of the sons of Israel, therefore you shall not bring this assembly into the land which I have given them" (Numbers 20:9-12).

Moving forward in the Old Testament, in 2 Samuel 16 the youngest son of Jesse, David, was anointed to be the next king of Israel after Saul. Years before he came to the throne, David demonstrated godly courage in his battle with the Philistine giant, Goliath. The account is usually considered a child's Bible class story, complete with the little song, but as Christian women there is an example in this account from which we can learn and make application in our lives.

The account of David going to see his brothers as they were camped against the Philistine army is recorded in 1 Samuel 17. When he arrived at the camp he heard the words of Goliath as he mocked the Hebrews and their God. David's reaction to this tirade was outrage from a heart filled with faith in God.

> Then David spoke to the men who were standing by him, saying, "What will be done for the man who kills this Philistine and takes away the reproach from Israel? For who is this uncircumcised Philistine, that he should taunt the armies of the living God?" (1 Samuel 17:26)

As David spoke to King Saul about confronting Goliath, his focus was on the power of God. His faith in God was unshakable.

> "The LORD who delivered me from the paw of the lion and from the paw of the bear, He will deliver me from the hand of this Philistine" (1 Samuel 17:37).

David's declaration to Goliath included that same laser focus on God's power and his own trust in Him.

> "You come to me with a sword, a spear, and a javelin, but I come to you in the name of the LORD of hosts, the God of the armies of Israel, whom you have taunted. This day the LORD will deliver you up into my hands, and I will strike you down and remove your head from you. And I will give the dead bodies of the army of the Philistines this day to the birds of the sky and the wild beasts of the earth, that all the earth may know that there is a God in Israel, and that all this assembly may know that the LORD does not deliver by sword or by spear; for the battle is the LORD'S and He will give you into our hands" (1 Samuel 17:45-47).

David's trust was unshakable because of his prior experience with the Lord's protection. His perspective was clear, uncluttered by adult pride in achievement; he knew the Lord would have the victory. His purpose in fighting was to conquer evil with the power and righteousness of God. There is much in this account we foolishly limit to our children's Bible classes. This true account can challenge the intensity and purity of our adult faith and courage.

The natural responses of a heart that is on intimate terms with God are outrage against that which opposes God, the impulse to expose it for the evil it is, and the desire to eliminate it by the power of God. In the New Testament Paul writes to the Ephesians:

> Do not participate in the unfruitful deeds of darkness, but instead even expose them (Ephesians 5:11).

If we can live in our society today and not feel continual outrage at the sin that has taken it over, we need to carefully consider what kind of faith is in our hearts. If we would have godly courage, we would be seeking ways to expose evil and overcome it with good, as opposed to living in peace with it.

In the New Testament we also see inspiring examples of godly courage. John the Baptist was a courageous prophet of God. His politically incorrect behavior speaking out against the immorality of Herod the Tetrarch got him killed. This account is in Matthew 14:1-12. John knew his purpose was to prepare the way for the Lord.

> He said, "I AM A VOICE OF ONE CRYING IN THE WILDERNESS, 'MAKE STRAIGHT THE WAY OF THE LORD,' as Isaiah the prophet said" (John 1:23).

John had seen God's Messiah; he had witnessed the endorsement of the Holy Spirit at Jesus' baptism, and he knew the prophecies were true. His purpose and his faith inspired him to continue to speak the truth and to push against evil publicly, even to his own detriment. He did not consider his imprisonment or death for the cause of righteousness too great a price to pay.

The apostle Peter is a human example of a person who struggled between godly and worldly courage. The Gospels lay out clearly his ongoing struggle with sin as a follower of Christ. His love for Christ and his faith did not prevent these mistakes, but they gave him perseverance in growth, which is probably the most important example for us. We give up on ourselves far too easily, deciding if we can't "get it right" after one or two tries, an undertaking is therefore too much for us. We use deficiencies we perceive in our personalities as excuses for not stepping out with godly courage. If we do step out and make mistakes and refuse to see them as learning experiences, we take ourselves out of service entirely. Satan loves it when he can get us to do this. Not only do we weaken our own faith when we withdraw into ourselves after a defeat, we may also discourage others from stepping out to serve God. One lesson I have learned is we never know who is watching us as we live out our Christian lives. The young woman quietly watching us struggle needs to know not only the fact we fell on our faces, she needs to see us have enough humility and trust in God to get up and keep trying to serve Him.

Peter twice made grand statements of commitment to the Lord, then promptly turned his back on his words, proving he didn't understand them fully.

> He said to them, "but who do you say that I am?" Simon Peter answered, "You are the Christ, the Son of the living God." And Jesus said to him, "Blessed are you, Simon Barjona, because flesh and blood did not reveal this to you, but My Father who is in heaven" (Matthew 16:16-17).

Just a few verses after this, Peter revealed his lack of spiritual focus.

> From that time Jesus began to show His disciples that He must go to Jerusalem, and suffer many things from the elders and chief priests and scribes, and be killed, and be raised up on the third day. Peter took Him aside and began to rebuke Him,

saying, "God forbid it, Lord! This shall never happen to you." But He turned and said to Peter, "Get behind Me, Satan! You are a stumbling block to Me; for you are not setting your mind on God's interests, but man's" (Matthew 16:21-23).

At the occasion of the Last Supper, as Jesus told his disciples about the coming suffering, He told them they would all fall away.

> But Peter said to Him, "Even though all may fall away because of You, I will never fall away." Jesus said to him, "Truly I say to you that this very night, before a rooster crows, you will deny Me three times." Peter said to Him, "Even if I have to die with You, I will not deny You." All the disciples said the same thing too (Matthew 26:33-35).

Perhaps it was a desire to prove to the Lord he meant what he said about never leaving him that caused Peter to cut off the ear of Malchus, the servant of the High Priest, as recorded in John 18:10. Peter was deep into emotionally motivated worldly courage, desperate to prove by his strength and goodness he would protect the Lord he loved. Read John 18:15-27, the complete account of Peter's denial of Jesus. His passion and love were not enough to overcome his fear when they were not accompanied by focus on Christ and faith that He was in control of events. We need to learn from this that our own courage, if motivated solely by emotions, will not carry us through crises. We must have the foundation of knowledge of the truth and trust in God to go with our God-given emotions!

Peter also demonstrated his humanity when he walked on the water to Jesus.

> And in the fourth watch of the night He came to them, walking on the sea. When the disciples saw Him walking on the sea, they were terrified, and said, "It is a ghost!" And they cried out in fear. But immediately Jesus spoke to them, saying, "Take courage, it is I; do not be afraid." Peter said to Him, "Lord, if it is You, command me to come to You on the water." And He said, "Come!" And Peter got out of the boat, and walked

on the water and came toward Jesus. But seeing the wind, he became frightened, and beginning to sink, he cried out, "Lord, save me!" Immediately Jesus stretched out His hand and took hold of him, and said to him, "You of little faith, why did you doubt?" (Matthew 14:25-31)

Peter did it; he walked on the water! He allowed Jesus to take him where he could never have gone alone! This must have been a heady experience. But Peter took his eyes off the Lord and started looking at the circumstances, the wind and the waves, and human thinking took over. His godly courage had allowed him a moment of freedom from his limitations. Worldly thinking brought them all crashing back. And worldly thinking dissolved his worldly passion for the Lord as he denied him three times.

> The Lord turned and looked at Peter. And Peter remembered the word of the Lord, how He had told him, "Before a rooster crows today, you will deny me three times." And he went out and wept bitterly (Luke 22:61-62).

If there was ever a time when we would give ourselves permission to give up on a mission, this type of circumstance would be it. How would we ever recover from having denied someone we loved so dearly in such a complete way? And yet, after His resurrection, Jesus restored Peter. Consider this conversation between Jesus and Peter:

> So when they had finished breakfast, Jesus said to Simon Peter, "Simon, son of John, do you love Me more than these?" He said to Him, "Yes, Lord; You know that I love You." He said to him, "Tend My lambs." He said to him again a second time, "Simon, son of John, do you love Me?" He said to Him, "Yes, Lord; You know that I love You." He said to him, "Shepherd My sheep." He said to him the third time, "Simon, son of John, do you love Me?" Peter was grieved because He said to him the third time, "Do you love Me?" And he said to Him, "Lord, You know all things; You know that I love You." Jesus said to him, "Tend My sheep. Truly, truly, I say to you, when you were younger, you

used to gird yourself and walk wherever you wished; but when you grow old, you will stretch out your hands and someone else will gird you, and bring you where you do not wish to go." Now this He said, signifying by what kind of death he would glorify God. And when He had spoken this, He said to him, "Follow Me!" (John 21:15-19)

From this moment on, Peter was a different man. He had seen the resurrected Lord; he was growing to understand the spiritual nature of the battle ahead. His love changed from worldly passion to spiritual fire, fed by the personal commission of the Lord on that beach. On the day of Pentecost Peter led the other apostles in presenting the first sermon. The first ten chapters of Acts detail much of his activity, including his encounter with the High Priest, the elders, and scribes.

> Then Peter, filled with the Holy Spirit, said to them, "Rulers and elders of the people, if we are on trial today for a benefit done to a sick man, as to how this man has been made well, let it be known to all of you and to all the people of Israel, that by the name of Jesus Christ the Nazarene, whom you crucified, whom God raised from the dead—by this name this man stands here before you in good health. He is the STONE WHICH WAS REJECTED by you, THE BUILDERS, but WHICH BECAME THE CHIEF CORNER stone. And there is salvation in no one else; for there is no other name under heaven that has been given among men by which we must be saved." Now as they observed the confidence of Peter and John and understood that they were uneducated and untrained men, they were amazed, and began to recognize them as having been with Jesus (Acts 4:8-13).

Though we are not called to lead a nation out of slavery or kill giants or preach to kings or organize the first congregation of the Lord's church, there are spiritual battles to be fought right where we are. As long as we live in this sinful world, there will be times when godly courage is required of us. We find this courage in complete faith in the power of God. We trust His power to use us in our broken state to do His work to expose evil and overcome it with good. Unlike the notoriety of Moses, David, John, and Peter, few people may ever know of our accomplishments. But the glory goes to God for anything we do, and if the battle we fight frees one soul from the slavery of sin, bringing them to Christ, then our service is worthwhile. May God give us His courage that we may ignore the fears and excuses in our heads and completely surrender ourselves to His service for His glory.

CHAPTER SIX **Questions for Discussion**

1. Who is the most courageous person you know? Share with the group what makes that person courageous.
2. Have you ever in your work for the Lord experienced His power allowing you to accomplish more than you imagined? Encourage the class with your experiences.
3. Have you noticed that in group situations, such as classes or working groups, if one person takes a positive stand others will follow?
4. What worldly motives get in the way of Christians having godly influences on people around them? Consider Moses' and Peter's early errors.
5. What positive motivations need to be in place to prevent us making the errors discussed in question 4?

CHAPTER SEVEN

Finding Courage (Part 2): The Surrender and Power of Prayer

No consideration of courageous Christian living can be complete without a study of the importance of prayer. We are familiar with the instruction to "pray without ceasing" (1 Thessalonians 5:17).

Christians often discuss the power of prayer. In this study we learn that the power of prayer is in the surrender it demands of us. When my father wanted to illustrate the contrast between effective and ineffective prayer, he used a sermon illustration similar to the following story: Two men went before the throne of God with all of their burdens carried in bags over their shoulders. Each of the men took his turn before the Father, unloading all of his burdens and laying them before the Father. Each detailed their concerns over the burdens one by one. When they had finished, one man carefully picked up each of his burdens, placed them back into his bag, hefted the bag on to his shoulder, and trudged out, back on his way. The other man picked up his empty bag and left his burdens at the throne of God, taking the Father's direction for how to proceed.

As we study some examples of prayerful people from the Bible, we will consider the aspect of surrendering to God. As we put into practice the deliberate action of surrendering to the will of the Father and exchanging our limited perspective to that of His eternal plan, He will work in ways we could never imagine.

Finding Courage (Part 2): The Surrender and Power of Prayer

> Be anxious for nothing, but in everything by prayer and supplication with thanksgiving let your requests be made known to God. And the peace of God, which surpasses all comprehension, shall guard your hearts and your minds in Christ Jesus (Philippians 4:6, 7).

As we develop the habit of thanksgiving for God's work, we learn to depend on Him more and have a greater sensitivity to observing God's activity in our world. This longer view brings us peace that people of the world cannot understand because of their belief that they are in control of their lives.

First Samuel begins with the account of Elkanah and his two wives, Hannah and Peninnah. In verse two of that chapter, it is revealed that Hannah was barren, while Peninnah had children. The situation resulted in much sorrow for Hannah. We read of the vow Hannah made to the Lord as she begged Him again for a son.

> She, greatly distressed, prayed to the LORD and wept bitterly. She made a vow and said, "O LORD of hosts, if You will indeed look on the affliction of Your maidservant and remember me, and not forget Your maidservant, but will give Your maidservant a son, then I will give him to the LORD all the days of his life, and a razor shall never come on his head" (1 Samuel 1:10-11).

We are told as the account goes on that Hannah's prayer continued long after the vow that she made to the Lord. She remained a long time praying silently before the Lord. Eli the priest was observing her as she prayed, and he became convinced she was drunk because of her behavior. When he went to rebuke her, however, Hannah's conversation with him proceeded as follows:

> "No, my lord; I am a woman oppressed in spirit; I have drunk neither wine nor strong drink, but I have poured out my soul before the LORD. Do not consider your maidservant as a worthless woman, for I have spoken until now out of my great concern and provocation. Then Eli answered and said, "Go in peace; and may the God of Israel grant your petition that you have asked of Him." She said, "Let your maidservant find favor in your sight."

So the woman went her way and ate, and her face was no longer sad (1 Samuel 1:15-18).

Hannah's actions after her time in prayer to the Lord show us her surrender to His will. Her conduct and attitude had changed from deep sorrow with fasting to getting on with her life. Further reading reveals once she returned home it was not long before Hannah conceived and bore Samuel. Any woman who has received a child after many fervent prayers can imagine the joy Hannah felt, and her love for this new flesh of her flesh. However, we see no evidence of any temptation for Hannah to go back on her vow. From the birth of the child she indicated her intention to bring the child and dedicate him at the temple as soon as he was weaned.

Hannah also prayed on the occasion of bringing Samuel to the temple. Her prayer was one of thanksgiving and praise for the power of God, as we read in 1 Samuel 2:1-10. Her actions prior to Samuel's birth and her praise upon dedicating him to a life of service to God reveal Hannah's surrender in prayer and in her life. Let us consider the prayerful habits of a great king of Israel.

Hezekiah inherited the throne at Jerusalem from his father Ahaz in 728 B.C. Unlike his father, Hezekiah loved God and was determined to obey Him as King David had. At 25 years of age he was mature enough to take the throne and effect reformation in Israel. He wasted no time; in the first month of his twenty-nine year reign he opened the doors of the temple and repaired them, as stated in 2 Chronicles 29:3. After that he gathered the Levites together and spoke to them about the sin of their tribe and the nation. He commanded them to cleanse the temple. In 2 Chronicles 29:10, Hezekiah informs the priestly tribe of his intention to restore the covenant with the Lord that the Israelites once had to turn away His wrath from the people. The King's commands were obeyed promptly; in sixteen days the years of neglect and blasphemy of previous kings was completely removed and the House of God was prepared for worship. (2 Chronicles 29:11-19)

Have you observed the energy and enthusiasm of faithful Christians who are in their twenties? That nearly boundless energy combined with growing knowledge and love for God is infectious. It can renew a spirit of hope and courage and imagination in older Christians as we observe them go after a task or a ministry. When I read of Hezekiah in this passage I imagine his passion for God igniting the hearts of those priests and people. Reading on in chapter 30 we see that Hezekiah's passion for worshipping God was not disorderly. He was highly concerned that the worship conform to the laws God had laid down. Unlike King Saul who sought to gain the people's favor by offering burnt offerings, Hezekiah left that duty to the priests. He used the opportunity of the worship to pray for his people; saying,

> "May the good LORD pardon everyone who prepares his heart to seek God, the LORD God of his fathers, though not according to the purification rules of the sanctuary" (2 Chronicles 30:18-19).

Verse 20 informs us that the Lord accepted Hezekiah's prayer and healed the people.

> All the assembly of Judah rejoiced, with the priests and the Levites and all the assembly that came from Israel, both the sojourners who came from the land of Israel and those living in Judah. So there was great joy in Jerusalem, because there was nothing like this in Jerusalem since the days of Solomon the son of David, king of Israel (2 Chronicles 30:25-26).

Hezekiah's work of restoring the nation of God went on for over a decade, and it is detailed in Chapter 31 of II Chronicles:

> Thus Hezekiah did throughout all Judah; and he did what was good, right and true before the LORD his God. Every work which he began in the service of the house of God in law and in commandment, seeking his God, he did with all his heart and prospered (2 Chronicles 31:20-21).

In these verses we see the surrender of Hezekiah in seeking God's will and the power of God in response.

Several years into Hezekiah's reign the king of Assyria, Sennacherib, brought his army to make war against Judah, moving toward Jerusalem. Hezekiah's response to this crisis is worth our study in considering his life of surrender to God. Second Chronicles 32 details the defenses Hezekiah ordered to be built up throughout the realm. He also sought to keep up the courage of his warriors.

> "Be strong and courageous, do not fear or be dismayed because of the king of Assyria nor because of all the horde that is with him; for the one with us is greater than the one with him. With him is only an arm of flesh, but with us is the LORD our God to help us and to fight our battles." And the people relied on the words of Hezekiah king of Judah (2 Chronicles 32:7-8).

Hezekiah's example of faith in God continued to inspire his people.

Sennacherib was intent upon winning the battle against Hezekiah and used psychological warfare as one of his weapons. He mounted a disinformation campaign against Hezekiah's faith and against the Lord God. Not only did he send his servants to Jerusalem to speak personally to Hezekiah's army, he wrote letters that insulted God and attempted to dissuade the general populace from believing in God. Sennacherib's servants read these letters aloud to the people of Jerusalem who were manning the walls. The mocking message was summarized:

> Now therefore, do not let Hezekiah deceive you or mislead you like this, and do not believe him, for no god of any nation or kingdom was able to deliver his people from my hand or from the hand of my fathers. How much less will your God deliver you from my hand? (2 Chronicles 32:15)

Second Kings 19 details Hezekiah's response to this potentially lethal emotional appeal from his enemy.

> Then Hezekiah took the letter from the hand of the messengers and read it, and he went up to the house of the LORD and spread

> it out before the LORD. Hezekiah prayed before the LORD and said, "Oh LORD, the God of Israel, who are enthroned above the cherubim, You are the God, You alone, of all the kingdoms of the earth. You have made heaven and earth. Incline Your ear, O LORD, and hear; open Your eyes, O LORD, and see; and listen to the words of Sennacherib, which he has sent to reproach the living God. Truly, O LORD, the kings of Assyria have devastated the nations and their lands and have cast their gods into the fire, for they were not gods but the work of men's hands, wood and stone. So they have destroyed them. Now, O LORD our God, I pray, deliver us from his hand that all the kingdoms of the earth may know that You alone, O LORD, are God" (2 Kings 19:14-19).

The youthful passion of this king for seeking God was not a fleeting emotional fad; it was the habit of his heart. He knew exactly what to do in a crisis...first thing...turn to God. Follow His command, believe in Him, and watch for His powerful response. Hezekiah was not disappointed.

> Then Isaiah the son of Amoz sent to Hezekiah, saying "Thus says the LORD, the God of Israel, 'Because you have prayed to Me about Sennacherib king of Assyria, I have heard you'...'Therefore thus says the LORD concerning the king of Assyria, "He will not come to this city or shoot an arrow there; and he will not come before it with a shield or throw up a siege ramp against it. By the way that he came, by the same he will return, and he shall not come to this city,"' declares the LORD. 'For I will defend this city to save it for My own sake for My servant David's sake.'" Then it happened that night that the angel of the LORD went out and struck 185,000 in the camp of the Assyrians; and when men rose early in the morning, behold, all of them were dead. So Sennacherib king of Assyria departed and returned home and lived at Nineveh. It came about as he was worshiping in the house of Nisroch his god, that Adrammelech and Sharezer killed him with the sword; and they escaped into the land of Ararat. And Esarhaddon his son became king in his place (2 Kings 19:20, 32-37).

As Hezekiah faced the end of his life with the sudden announcement from Isaiah that he was to die, he turned to God first in prayer. He poured out his sorrow to God, as recorded in II Kings 20:1-11. This was one of those prayers that was answered immediately; Isaiah had not even left the house when God instructed him to return to Hezekiah with the news that he would live fifteen years more. Hezekiah displayed mistaken pride toward the end of his life. However, because of his faithfulness in prayer and his determination to live in obedience to God, he was rewarded with a peaceful life.

In Philippians 2:5-8 we read about the surrendering spirit of Jesus.

> Have this attitude in yourselves which was also in Christ Jesus, who, although He existed in the form of God, did not regard equality with God a thing to be grasped, but emptied Himself, taking the form of a bond-servant, and being made in the likeness of men. Being found in appearance as a man, He humbled Himself by becoming obedient to the point of death, even death on a cross.

As surrender is an ongoing process for us, so it was for Christ. The Greek word for "emptied" in this case literally means to "make of none effect, to make of no reputation."[1] All that Christ was as God He had to set aside to become the One Sacrifice that was acceptable for our sin. He told His disciples in Matthew 20:28, "...the Son of Man did not come to be served, but to serve, and to give His life a ransom for many."

Jesus' prayer in John 17 is that of an obedient son completely focused on the will of the Father. In the first few verses, Jesus prays for Himself, asking God to glorify Him. But we see that it is not for Jesus' own exaltation that He prays. Rather, He asks for glorification that God might be exalted, that the plan might be fulfilled to offer salvation to the world.

> "...Father, the hour has come; glorify Your Son, that the Son may glorify You, even as You gave Him authority over all flesh, that

to all whom You have given Him, He may give eternal life. This is eternal life, that they may know You, the only true God, and Jesus Christ whom You have sent. I glorified You on the earth, having accomplished the work which You have given Me to do. Now, Father, glorify Me together with Yourself, with the glory which I had with You before the world was" (John 17:1-5).

Jesus' prayers in Gethsemane rend our hearts as we imagine Him there, knowing in detail the agony He was facing in only hours. The greatest of all agony being separation from the Father as He became the sin of all humanity so that He could to atone for us. Yet His prayers were humble declarations of surrender.

"...My Father, if it is possible, let this cup pass from Me; yet not as I will, but as You will...My Father, if this cannot pass away unless I drink it, Your will be done" (Matthew 26:39, 42).

The beautiful book of Acts begins with the ascension of Jesus and the return of the Apostles and disciples to Jerusalem to wait for the baptism of the Holy Spirit that was promised in Acts 1:5. The first task for the apostles was to select a replacement for Judas. We see their surrender to the Father as we read their prayer:

"You, Lord, who know the hearts of all men, show which one of these two You have chosen to occupy this ministry and apostleship from which Judas turned aside to go to his own place" (Acts 1:24-25).

There was no politics involved in this decision, only prayer.

As the apostles began to carry out the commission given to them by Jesus, it was not long before they encountered opposition and persecution. Acts 4 details the first of many confrontations between Peter and John and the rulers and elders and scribes of the Jews. Their godly courage, fueled by unshakable faith and the power of the Holy Spirit enabled the apostles to answer this group with strength and honesty. When they were released to their companions, their first action was a prayer.

"O Lord, it is YOU WHO MADE THE HEAVEN AND THE EARTH

AND THE SEA, AND ALL THAT IS IN THEM, who by the Holy Spirit, through the mouth of our father David Your servant, said, 'WHY DID THE GENTILES RAGE, AND THE PEOPLES DEVISE FUTILE THINGS? THE KINGS OF THE EARTH TOOK THEIR STANDS, AND THE RULERS WERE GATHERED TOGETHER AGAINST THE LORD AND AGAINST HIS CHRIST.' For truly in this city there were gathered together against Your holy servant Jesus, whom You anointed, both Herod and Pontius Pilate, along with the Gentiles and the peoples of Israel, to do whatever Your hand and Your purpose predestined to occur. And now, Lord, take note of their threats, and grant that Your bond-servants may speak Your word with all confidence, while You extend Your hand to heal, and signs and wonders take place through the name of Your holy servant Jesus" (Acts 4:24-30).

These men were not shaken by the treatment they had just received; they knew the Power behind them was God. They went to Him in prayer and praise, asking for His will to be done and for confidence to continue doing His will. This was one of those prayers answered immediately!

And when they had prayed, the place where they had gathered together was shaken, and they were all filled with the Holy Spirit and began to speak the word of God with boldness (Acts 4:31).

As the borders of God's kingdom expanded, prayer continued to be important.

Now when the apostles in Jerusalem heard that Samaria had received the word of God, they sent them Peter and John, who came down and prayed for them that they might receive the Holy Spirit. For he had not yet fallen upon any of them; they had simply been baptized in the name of the Lord Jesus. Then they began laying their hands on them, and they were receiving the Holy Spirit (Acts 8:14-17).

Paul's ministry was also punctuated by prayer.

While they were ministering to the Lord and fasting, the Holy Spirit said, "Set apart for Me Barnabas and Saul for the work to which I have called them." Then, when they had fasted and prayed and laid their hands on them, they sent them away (Acts 13:2-3).

In the midst of persecution and imprisonment, Acts 16:25 describes Paul engaging in prayer and song with Silas, again with immediate results!

In his inspired writings to the churches, Paul always indicated his prayerfulness for the brethren. In the first chapter of Paul's letter to the Ephesians we glimpse his priority in prayer.

> For this reason I too, having heard of the faith in the Lord Jesus which exists among you and your love for all the saints, do not cease giving thanks for you, while making mention of you in my prayers; that the God of our Lord Jesus Christ, the Father of glory, may give to you a spirit of wisdom and of revelation in the knowledge of Him. I pray that the eyes of your heart may be enlightened, so that you will know what is the hope of His calling, what are the riches of the glory of His inheritance in the saints, and what is the surpassing greatness of His power toward us who believe (Ephesians 1:15-19).

Paul also told the Christians in Thessalonica:

> We give thanks to God always for all of you, making mention of you in our prayers; constantly bearing in mind your work of faith and labor of love and steadfastness of hope in our Lord Jesus Christ in the presence of our God and Father... (1 Thessalonians 1:2-3)

Paul gave thanks for the brothers and sisters in every congregation. Imagine the good that could result if we would open our hearts to God in thanksgiving for the Christians with whom we attend church!

James writes about prayer in the letter that bears his name:

> Is anyone among you suffering? Then he must pray. Is anyone cheerful? He is to sing praises. Is anyone among you sick? Then he must call for the elders of the church and they are to pray over him, anointing him with oil in the name of the Lord; and

the prayer offered in faith will restore the one who is sick, and the Lord will raise him up, and if he has committed sins, they will be forgiven him. Therefore, confess your sins to one another, and pray for one another so that you may be healed. The effective prayer of a righteous man can accomplish much (James 5:13-16).

As New Testament Christians, these scriptures and so many others of command and example in the Bible speak to us, admonishing us to make prayer and surrender a daily part of our lives.

As we consider Moses as he stood before Pharaoh, Elijah as he stood against the prophets of Baal, Daniel as he prayed in the lions' den, Stephen as he was stoned, Paul as he stood before Caesar, and the many other great heroes in the pages of the Bible, we see a common thread: surrender. Whether or not their prayers are written down for us, we know that these all surrendered their own desires and lives to the will of the Father. Their minds and hearts were singularly focused on God, on doing His will. We know they were not perfect servants because in the Bible we read of their weaknesses as well as their strengths. However, we know that in spite of their imperfections God chose them, God used them, and to the extent that they surrendered to Him they brought glory to God as they fulfilled their part of His divine plan. In the same way, today we have opportunities before us to obediently serve God. Once we have surrendered ourselves and our worries to God in prayer, may we rise up with faithful courage to grasp those opportunities, recognizing that His power is shown to others in the work He enables us to do.

CHAPTER SEVEN **Questions for Discussion**

1. If you have a favorite passage on the subject of prayer or a favorite prayer in the Bible, share it with the class.
2. Why would our all-knowing God desire that we pray to Him?
3. How would you respond to the statement, "There are some things too small for us to pray to God about"?

4. Has there been an episode in your life in which God did not give you the answer to prayer you were desiring? Have you been able to see a long-term result from that?
5. How does surrendering to God help us be courageous?

Reference

1. Strong, James, 2010. The New Strong's Expanded Exhaustive Concordance of the Bible. Published by Thomas Nelson Publishers, Nashville, TN.

CHAPTER EIGHT

Courage in Marriage: Choose to Submit to Your Husband

In the first five chapters of this book, we revealed alarming trends in history and culture that have contributed to serious problems in our society. These problems exist not only in our country, but in global society. In chapters six and seven, we studied Scripture to consider developing courage to effect change in this troubled society. Now we will consider some important areas where courageous living and teaching is needed from Christian women. Readers may be surprised given the secular nature of the information shared at the beginning of the obedience to Scripture rather than concepts founded on modern behavioral theories and ideas. However, given the problems that have resulted in part from individual Christians choosing to adhere to secular teachings over the last 180 years, it is my belief that we will have the most revolutionary effect on both our own and future generations by practicing and teaching deliberate obedience to the Bible.

The Apostle Paul was described by opponents in Acts 17:6 as being part of a small number of men who had "turned the world upside down" with his teaching. He was one of only twelve men who revolutionized the world with the gospel. As we live and teach our faith to those around us daily, God can use us to revitalize not only our own culture, but the world. Let us now courageously and joyously face the New Testament teachings directed to wives! Let us contemplate how to put these teachings into practice in our lives, and let us consider practical ways we can pass them on to the next generation of Christian women. The emphasis of these topics will be a review to mature Christian women. To younger Christians this may be material that has only been presented from a negative perspective, if at all. We can all benefit from studying the commands of God to women and teaching them to others.

As women who desire to live by the authority of the Bible, we are faced first with the teachings of God about His order of authority among Himself, men, and women.

> But I want you to understand that Christ is the head of every man, and the man is the head of a woman, and God is the head of Christ (1 Corinthians 11:3).

As those who profess belief in God as Author and Creator of the universe, we must accept that He set this order in existence as He set the planets in orbit of the sun. We live in His universe; we need not only to live by His rules, but we also need to courageously model joyful obedience to this order of authority to our congregations and to our communities.

> Wives, be subject to your own husbands, as to the Lord. For the husband is the head of the wife, as Christ also is the head of the church, He Himself being the Savior of the body. But as the church is subject to Christ, so also the wives ought to be to their husbands in everything (Ephesians 5:22-24).

The Greek word that describes the instruction "be subject to" means to consciously choose to put oneself under another as to a military commander.[3]

In chapter 3 we discussed the philosophy of modern feminism and how it has demoralized our culture. Any man and woman who choose to have a marriage that is pleasing to God place themselves at odds with a society gone mad with selfishness. As I heard in a recent sermon, "The 'Me' generation has given birth to the 'Me, Me, Me!' generation."[2] In this atmosphere it requires faithful courage for a woman to choose to put herself into subjection to her husband. A figure to help illustrate the concept of submission would be two people getting into a car together to go somewhere. We notice that there is only one steering wheel in a car. The person in the driver's seat makes the decisions as to where the car will go and at what speed it will travel. The person in the passenger seat is along for the ride. Perhaps the person in the passenger seat will give directions to get to the destination or make comments on the speed of the driver, but ultimately the driver makes all the decisions. If the driver does not know the way to the destination and chooses not to listen to the passenger who does know, the car will be lost and the driver will appear foolish. However, the passenger cannot stage a takeover of the car without risking a serious accident. A car with two steering wheels and sets of pedals on the floor will not get anywhere. Likewise, in a marriage when the husband and the wife both attempt to lead, the relationship cannot go anywhere. Jesus once observed,

> "If a house is divided against itself, that house will not be able to stand" (Mark 3:25).

Subjection is a daily decision for a woman. A critical point we need to consider according to Scripture is the decision to submit is not made based upon the fitness of the husband. I believe one reason for this could be that there is an assumption that careful consideration and preparation went into the decision of whom the woman would marry. We studied in chapter 3 the example of the arranged marriage of Rebekah and Isaac. Abraham sent his servant to his own homeland in search of a worthy woman for his son, and that servant prayed for God's guidance. Abraham's kinsmen, because they knew of Abraham's character and assumed that his son would have been raised to those same high standards, had no problem with the proposal that their daughter would go away and marry this man they had never met. According to the *Encyclopedia of Gender and Society*, as quoted in Wikipedia in May 2014, arranged marriages not unlike this one were commonly practiced throughout the world until the 18th century. In the United States the concept of arranged marriage is assumed to indicate a forced, abusive situation. However, the practice of parents or church authorities having partial or complete control over the pairing of men and women is still common in South and Southeast Asia, Africa, the Middle East, and Latin America. Also, the accepted practice of "assisted" or "quasi-arranged" marriages, where the man and woman are introduced to each other and after a period of courting, make their own choice whether to marry, continues to be popular in the countries of Japan, Latin America, Africa, and South and East Asia. Arranged marriages are not a guarantee of a happy, life-long marriage, and it is not my intent to advocate the practice. But where there is careful consideration and mature preparation for marriage, it is easier for the man and woman to have a good relationship.

As courageous mothers we can study biblical examples of godly husbands with our daughters , and help them to bypass worldly values and seek relationships with Christian young men who will follow God's commands for husbands. If they have chosen a worthy man for a husband, though submitting to him will at times be difficult, it will be far less difficult. We can show them what submission looks like in a Christian marriage; that it is a joyful thing to obey God's command in this area.

Another command to wives is that they respect their husbands, as stated in Ephesians 5:33. To respect someone does not require us to always agree with them. It does require that we honor them for their leadership position. Again, we notice that the command is not conditional on the husband being worthy of respect. Paul relates a command to the husband in that same verse, but neither command is conditional. If we would be obedient to our Lord, we will respect our husbands because He told us to do it.

The context of 1 Peter 3:1-6 describes again the respectful

behavior wives are to exhibit for their husbands. Consider the last verse in that section:

> ...just as Sarah obeyed Abraham, calling him lord, and you have become her children if you do what is right without being frightened by any fear (1 Peter 3:6).

Fear is probably the first emotion that comes into the mind of a married woman at the thought of submitting completely to her husband. It is all well and good to talk about arranged marriages in the Bible and the ideal of marrying a man prepared to be a spiritual and physical leader of his family, but what about the women who find themselves married to someone who is not prepared to be that kind of leader? Does that mean that these commands do not apply to the modern woman? If we would be faithful Christians, we cannot accept that thought. We know Jesus said in John 10:10 that He came that we might enjoy abundant life. We also know that God does not give us more than we can bear, as stated in 1 Corinthians 10:13. We are left with trying to figure out how to obey the commands to submit to and respect our husbands. The depth of that subjection is described at the end of Ephesians 5:22, "...as to the Lord." We can only choose to yield our own authority to that of our imperfect husbands when we have first yielded the throne of our hearts to the Lord. We studied that obedient surrender in the hearts of God's people gave them courage to do great things. That same surrender, based on the trust that God will provide, gives us the strength to let go of the reins of our families and hand them back to the men God intended to lead them. Matthew 6:25-33 reminds us that if we make serving God our first priority, He will provide everything we need. Feeling a desperate need to lead our families when it seems that our husbands cannot do the job often comes from a desire for financial security. This challenging, yet beautiful context encourages us not to give in to that desperation.

What does this surrender look like? It is going to be different for every woman. Husbands have varying priorities, and just as it takes husband and wife working together to make a successful family spiritually; more often than not it takes both spouses to pay the bills. As Christian sisters we can be of greatest encouragement to one another in the area of submission to husbands by recognizing that how individual families function is up to the husband. It is not ours to approve of the various styles of families we see among brothers and sisters in Christ. Women have a divine example of what surrender looks like in Christ. When we feel as wives we are being asked to give up too much, we would do well to remember this passage,

> Have this attitude in yourselves which was also in Christ Jesus, who, although He existed in the form of God, did not regard equality with God a thing to be grasped, but emptied Himself, taking the form of a bond-servant, and being made in the likeness of men. Being found in appearance as a man, He humbled Himself by becoming obedient to the point of death, even death on a cross (Philippians 2:5-8).

For the married woman service to God is bound up with her relationship with her husband, as Paul points out at the end of 1 Corinthians 7:34. In a world where all forms of entertainment glorify lives for men and women which are endless streams of relationships based on self-gratification, the nurturing of a healthy, lasting marriage which fulfills God's plan must be a deliberate, daily priority for the Christian wife.

Teaching young Christian women about the elements of lifelong marriages is so critical for mothers and older Christian women that Titus 2:4 reads in part,

> ...so that they may encourage the young women to love their husbands,

We need to understand that the Greek definition of the word *encourage* is "to admonish, to exhort earnestly," and is also interpreted "train."[3] This is a process that implies time and effort.

In 2008, Malcom Gladwell published the book, *Outliers, the Story of Success*. This book is famous in part because of a study he details done in the 1990s at the Berlin Academy of Music to determine the roles of talent and practice in the mastery of playing the violin. That study, combined with studies in other contexts, led to the following observation,

> "The emerging picture from such studies is that ten thousand hours of practice is required to achieve the level of mastery associated with being a world-class expert-in anything." Neurologist Daniel Levitin.[1]

As Christians we are not competing for the title of "world class expert." However, given the disturbing state of marriages in our communities and churches, can we deny that more time is needed to teach our daughters how to be good wives? Some other questions this thinking may provoke are, "How do we train our young girls to be good Christian wives? What do we tell them?" In addition to what they observe in our relationship with our husbands and support of biblical teaching, there are some things we can tell them. The following observations are basic and by no means exhaustive, but are intended as suggested starting points in teaching.

Since every marriage is made up of individuals, one healthy marriage can look quite different from another. Having observed several successful marriages and others that dissolved, it appears there are some common characteristics that are evidence of work done to stay together. The first is that obedience and surrender to God are the top priority for the woman. The most ideal and harmonious situation is when the husband and wife are both committed Christians, but I have a dear friend whose husband has never become a Christian in spite of her example. She patiently obeys God and submits to her husband and nurtures their relationship. I have known other marriages where the husband became a Christian after more than 40 years of married life because of the wife's patient example. But if the woman is not a faithful Christian it is much more difficult for the man to remain faithful. In 1 Kings 11:1-4 we are told that Solomon, the wisest man of all time, had 700 wives and 300 concubines, and they led his heart away from God by the end of his life. Many husbands today find that it only takes one wife to do the same thing to their faith as they strive to please a woman who refuses to humble herself to God.

Another characteristic in successful marriages is that the husband and wife choose to be each other's best friends. This is not easy because husbands and wives have different definitions of what makes a good friend. In the case of couples who have opposite personalities, it can take years to come to this relationship, but as Christians successfully navigate trials together and see God's work in their marriage and the lives of their children, they can become best friends. The determination must be made by each spouse that the needs and desires of the other, and spending time with them will be more important than the relationship with any other friend. Best friends want to be together. In the cultures of the Bible times, it was not common for men and women not married to each other to have casual conversations with each other. Perhaps because of this custom, we do not see specific commands regarding outside associations of husbands and wives. This is an area where spouses need to use the wisdom of understanding that one level of intimacy leads to another. Married best friends do not choose to be alone with friends of the opposite sex. They do not text or engage in other electronic communication with friends of the opposite sex without the inclusion of their mate, and they don't look up ex-boyfriends or ex-girlfriends on social media. Best friends support each other, they do not embarrass each other; they may tease but they never throw each other under the bus. Couples have different levels of what is considered funny and what is embarrassing, but in all cases married best friends concentrate on building up the best in each other.

The Christian wife seeking to please God will work with her husband so that each spouse may grow beyond his or her faults. However, she does not allow her relationship to be eroded by concentrating on her husband's faults or comparing him to other men. It is important for wives to choose what entertainment they see, listen to, and engage in, to make sure it does not cause them to become discontented with their husbands. The romantic hero with the ripped muscles who sweeps in from a day of saving the world with a rose, smooth words, and passionate embrace for his heroine must not be compared with the weary husband, home from a difficult day that produced no progress at work, who has difficulty noticing his wife's new hairstyle. When the husband and wife both work outside the home, supportive nurturing of the relationship becomes even more difficult as both are worn down by the demands of the job and responsibilities at home. But a kind word of understanding and appreciation whenever possible is even more important during those stressful times.

A truly wise wife will learn to see the upside of her husband's flaws. A man who does not easily spend money may be a man who is committed to being a good steward of God's blessings and saving for future emergencies. A man who spends money freely may be a man of great faith in God, an example of trust who generously gives to provide joy for his wife, family, and others, believing that God will provide what is needed in the future. Finally, there are the flaws that a man cannot overcome successfully due to previous abuses or trauma. As more of our veterans return from war with Post-Traumatic Stress Disorder or Traumatic Brain Injury, there are more spouses who will need to be supportive and patient with conditions that cannot be changed. Traditional vows usually include the phrase, "in sickness and in health." Not all illnesses are obvious, and some are discovered after the wedding ceremony is over. But a woman who has surrendered her will to the Lord can receive the strength she needs to be faithful to a husband whose need for her is greater than she expected, and she can trust the Lord to fulfill her needs.

A wife who is working to nurture her marriage and be submissive to her husband will be thoughtful in how she communicates to him. The Old Testament offers us several examples of wives whose communication to their husbands had lasting effects on their marriages. In Esther 1, there is a stark contrast in the communication of King Ahasuerus' wives. The first Queen, Vashti, responded to her lord's command that she dance for his guests with physical defiance which humiliated him, and resulted in her losing her position and being banished. Esther, however, when faced with the need to initiate a conversation with the king in respect to the plot to destroy the Jews, chose a different strategy. In chapters 4-7 of Esther, review how she approached her husband with humility above all, and respect, and she gave him good reason to listen to her request by serving him great dinners. Abigail, the wife of Nabal, also showed wisdom in her dealings with her husband, as described in 1 Samuel 25. First of all, her humble, yet proactive response of bringing food to David saved him from slaughtering Nabal and his household. Then, her well-timed words to Nabal, in private, after he finished his party, went straight to his heart. Her patience, discernment, and diplomacy were rewarded when she was made one of David's wives. David's first wife, Michal, did not show the same wisdom. In 2 Samuel 6 is the account of her public rebuke to her husband upon his completion of returning the Ark of the Covenant to Jerusalem. Her cynical condemnation of her husband in front of their servants ended the intimacy between her and David, as the Scripture reads in verse 23, "Michal the daughter of Saul had no child to the day of her death."

Christian wives are also concerned with meeting their

husband's sexual needs. In the Garden of Eden, Adam and Eve were told to be fruitful and multiply. The physical relationship between husband and wife is discussed by Paul in 1 Corinthians 7:1-4. In this context the purpose for that intimacy goes beyond creating children. The regular, intimate contact between husband and wife is described in this context as the way for each to avoid sexual immorality. The culture of societies since ancient times has been permeated with obsession with sexual fulfillment, making the stewardship of Christian husband and wife of each other's sexual purity a sacred trust.

Partners in marriages that last are good forgivers. Even though a young man and woman approach marriage with love and hope, eventually hurt and despair creep in. The devil is always finding ways to entice one or the other or both into selfish sin. There is no such thing as a perfect marriage just as there is no such thing as a perfect Christian. There is no family on this earth that is not dysfunctional because of the reality of sin. We are all imperfect souls in need of the grace of God. However, as hurt Christians remember the sacrifice made for them by Jesus and the commitment they made individually to remain faithful to Him, they can find forgiveness for an erring spouse who repents. A couple who realizes they have lost their way in the world can find that the same determination they make to return to Christ can help them remake their marriage, even coping with the consequences of their lapse.

A popular meme on social media is a picture of an elderly couple who have been asked how they remained married for 50, 60, or 70 years. Although the picture may be of different couples, with different numbers of years married, the answer to the question is always the same: "Because we lived in a time when if something was broken you fixed it, you didn't throw it away." I have never seen an author of this, but it is a pointed secular instruction to all of us who choose to marry. Yes, there are situations where one spouse insists on forsaking the marriage vows or when safety concerns make it impossible for living together to continue. But the command from Jesus is clear:

> "So they are no longer two, but one flesh. What therefore God has joined together, let no man separate" (Matthew 19:6).

The faithful Christian will do everything possible not to be the one who seeks a divorce.

> An excellent wife, who can find? For her worth is far above jewels. The heart of her husband trusts in her, and he will have no lack of gain. She does him good and not evil all the days of her life (Proverbs 31:10-12).

The courageous Christian wife will respect and submit joyfully to her husband because she has first submitted joyfully to her Lord. She will make her husband her first priority after the Lord, and she will work daily to benefit him. She will consider him her best friend, and in addition to whatever her other work involves, she will work daily to keep her marriage strong. She will also seek every opportunity to teach these principles both verbally and by example to her daughters and the younger women with whom she has influence, to benefit their lives and marriages in the future.

CHAPTER EIGHT Questions for Discussion

1. Discuss subtle messages in our culture to discourage women from submitting to their husbands.
2. Discuss methods of helping girls and single women to consider spiritual characteristics in potential husbands at least as important as physical characteristics.
3. If someone had told you before you married your husband about his trait that irritates you the most, is it likely you would have listened?
4. How does understanding the command that married women are supposed to submit to their husbands have any importance to the single woman in the church?

5. Does showing our husbands the agape love outlined in 1 Corinthians 13:4-7 teach us anything about the love God has for us?

References

1. Gladwell, Malcom, 2008. Outliers, the Story of Success, (p. 40). Published by Little, Brown, and Company, Hachette Book Group, New York, NY.
2. Ron White Sermon at Wasatch church of Christ, February 2014, description of the "Me, Me, Me!" generation.
3. Strong, James, 2010. The New Strong's Expanded Exhaustive Concordance of the Bible. Published by Thomas Nelson Publishers, Nashville, TN.

CHAPTER NINE

Courage as Mothers: Choose to Train Your Children

For generations we have been trained to begin new phases of our lives with help from the "experts." Perhaps nowhere is this tendency as blatant as becoming a mother for the first time. The first-time mom reads *What to Expect When You're Expecting* and checks everything off as her pregnancy progresses. She carefully considers the pros and cons of cloth diapers and breast feeding and when to introduce solid food. It is natural and admirable for us to study to be the best moms we can be. The question is, which "expert" advice will we research on parenting? Bookstore shelves sink under the weight of parenting books for managing the smallest to the most significant challenges of parenting.

The Creator of the universe has instructions for parenting, just as He does for marriage, because He understands we need to be taught. In Titus 2:4, after telling the older women to train the younger women to love their husbands, Paul tells them they are also to train them to love their children. Older women make good instructors on marriage and parenting because of the successes we have enjoyed, but also because of the mistakes we have made in these relationships. It is the mistakes we have made that prove that God's will for our lives is the best way to live. One of the saddest news stories of late has been the discovery of the bodies of six infants in a garage in a typical suburban neighborhood. The subsequent arrest of and confession by the mother of those children whom she strangled impressed on me the terrible reality this woman missed God's directions for mothers. Her innocent children paid the highest price for that lack of training.

The ultimate model of parenting is the example of God. His regard for His children was constant; His behavior toward them was consistent; His sacrifice for them was complete. He was never too busy to meet needs. He did not start up the world and create man only to decide He was bored and choose to do something else. God never betrayed the trust of His people; He gave clear directions and clear promises of consequences, and He always followed through. He offered observant children repeated opportunities to learn what his expectations were through the prophets in the Old Testament and the principles of His new covenant in the New Testament. In spite of repeated rebellion of His creation, God the Father offers us an opportunity to take advantage of His grace because of the sacrifice of Jesus the Son. He gave us His Word in terms we could understand and told us exactly how to obey Him. As we study these aspects of God's "parenting style" in the Bible, we can gain insight into ways we can become the courageous mothers He would have us to be.

As our Eternal Father, God's regard for His children is constant. We see this first in the creation account of Genesis.

> Then God said, "Let Us make man in Our image, according to Our likeness; and let them rule over the fish of the sea and over the birds of the sky and over the cattle and over all the earth, and over every creeping thing that creeps on the earth." God created man in His own image, in the image of God He created him; male and female He created them. God blessed them; and God said to them, "Be fruitful and multiply, and fill the earth, and subdue it; and rule over the fish of the sea and over the birds of the sky and over every living thing that moves on the earth." Then God said, "Behold, I have given you every plant yielding seed that is on the surface of all the earth, and every tree which has fruit yielding seed; it shall be food for you; and to every beast of the earth and to every bird of the sky and to

every thing that moves on the earth which has life, I have given every green plant for food;" and it was so. (Genesis 1:26-30)

God created man on the sixth day of creation, after He had first created a suitable habitat for mankind. He gave man dominion over all creation; it was all meant for man's use, that he might grow and thrive. As moms we are concerned with providing safe, comfortable places for our children and making sure we provide good nutrition for them as they grow. Literature is readily available on the topics of safety and nutrition for children. An important thing to consider for the Christian mother is how well we are feeding and nurturing our children spiritually. Are we making sure they are growing up in an environment that is safe spiritually? The best way for us to begin to provide a safe spiritual environment for them is by making sure our own spiritual environment is a healthy one. Our children will quickly spot our inconsistencies, and they will argue against us when they begin to make choices of their own. They need to observe our daily habits of Bible study and prayer and see our choice of entertainment which encourage our obedience to God. Understanding that all their lives they will have to choose between God and the world, just as we have to, are we filling our own minds as well as theirs with the truth of God's existence, His Word, His power, and His love for us? Do we help them fill their little minds with those things that are, as Paul wrote in Philippians 4:8, "true, honorable, right, pure, lovely, of good reputation, excellence, and praiseworthy"? Do we remember what Jesus said about the importance of the things in our hearts?

> "But the things that proceed out of the mouth come from the heart, and those defile the man. For out of the heart come evil thoughts, murders, adulteries, fornications, false witness, slanders" (Matthew 15:18-19).

Most of us are familiar with the exhortation Moses gave to the children of Israel:

"These words, which I am commanding you today, shall be on your heart. You shall teach them diligently to your sons and shall talk of them when you sit in your house and when you walk by the way and when you lie down and when you rise up" (Deuteronomy 6:6-7).

It may seem like stating the obvious to say this passage emphasizes the importance of repetition in our teaching to our children. When I think of the alarming number of young people I know who have left the church as soon as they left their homes, though, perhaps as parents we would do well to pay increased attention to repeating spiritual teaching! This requires more from us than presenting the little ones faithfully at the door of their Bible class twice a week. We accept the premise that for them to become proficient in sports or school or music or drama requires many hours of practice, and we are willing to change the family routine in support of that practice. In fact, I know of a family who did not attend Bible class on Sunday morning because their daughter's sports practice was that morning, and they did not want to neglect her learning those skills! Just as our kids repeat the basics in warm-up exercises and dribbling basketballs, they need to repeat the basics in spiritual skills. Speaking with kindness, forgiving others, telling the truth, praying when they are worried and afraid or are thankful and happy are just a few examples of spiritual skills with which children need deliberate practice. Just as they face increased challenges in school with tests in math and science and spelling, they need to face challenges to help them learn what the Bible says about creation and the power of God and the truth of the historical accounts of the Gospels. Where will they learn these skills, where will they become grounded in Bible truths, if not at home? As moms we hope that as our children go through school, ambition will ignite and they will follow paths leading them to a productive life physically. Do we treasure the same hope in our hearts for their souls? Do we pray for their spiritual development? As we help them plan the classes they will take in junior high and high school in preparation for college, do we plan how we will teach them spiritual truths?

The home is the place where children learn how to be a part of a physical family. The Christian home is the place where children learn how to be faithful Christians for the one hundred sixty-five hours of the week they are not sitting in a church service. Ideally this instruction will come from a father and mother who began having discussions about the spiritual growth of their children before they were born and are in agreement. Much emphasis has been given in previous chapters to the importance of husbands and fathers, and nothing in this chapter should be construed as implying mothers are exclusively responsible for raising Christian children. However, as has been stated, the message of this book is for women; no effort is being made in these pages to instruct men on their roles. There are many women who for various reasons are left with the sole responsibility for teaching the children in their care. These women must walk closely with the Lord in dependence on Him for energy, strength, wisdom, courage, humor, and compassion in leading their children. Their Christian brothers and sisters have a responsibility to be sensitive to areas where they can offer support. We know of at least one Christian mother in the New Testament who was, with her own mother, responsible for the spiritual growth of her son, the young evangelist Timothy.

One of the parenting philosophies that has been around since my parents were rearing me is the idea that purports children are innocent; they have an inborn knowledge of what is good and do not require training in right and wrong. This worldly belief is in opposition to the Word of God. Solomon, the wisest king of Israel, was inspired to write several proverbs directly bearing on this philosophy. If the examples of Adam and Eve, Cain and Abel, Abraham and Sarah are not enough, consider these Scriptures:

...a foolish son is a grief to his mother (Proverbs 10:1). A fool rejects his father's discipline, but he who regards reproof is sensible (Proverbs 15:5). Foolishness is bound up in the heart of a child; the rod of discipline will remove it far from him (Proverbs 22:15). He who withholds his rod hates his son, but he who loves him disciplines him diligently (Proverbs 13:24).

In this last verse, the term *rod* is footnoted in the NASB as "correction." Our modern interpretation of *rod* can conjure images of a child being beaten in an abusive way. We understand, however, that correction can take different forms. And the term *discipline* in our society is often used to describe bringing either our minds, emotions, or bodies under specific control. As adults we understand we need teaching and practice to attain success in life; we ought not to shrink from the idea of our children requiring correction and discipline to be successful and productive adults. As courageous Christian mothers we should advocate for productive discipline. We want to bring our young ones to an appreciation for the needs of people around them. We want them to have appropriate respect for earthly authority so they are capable of submitting their wills to God at the right time. A toddler who makes a habit of yelling at his mother or who strikes her when she attempts to correct him will likely not respect future teachers. As this child grows, he has little chance of understanding why he should submit to a God whose teachings get in his way of satisfying his pleasures in this life. Productive discipline will involve us treating our children with kindness and consistency. We will follow through with promised consequences for deliberate disobedience. We will praise them for positive behavior and growth. We will support them and let them reach forward with new skills. We will encourage them to learn lessons from failure, just as we must.

As Christian women, when we become mothers we take on a lifelong role. Because of the freedoms we enjoy in our culture, we will be tempted away from our families with many distractions.

But if we would be dedicated to our children's highest good, we will keep those distractions to a minimum. If we are fortunate to have our husbands with us, the choices we make about activities will complement priorities made with them. Our behavior with our children will be consistent; we will take the time to teach them and teach them again and again in ways effective for them until they show understanding. We understand we only have a few years with our children before the world's influence in the forms of school, friends, and entertainment will compete for their attention to us. Therefore, we, like Timothy's mother and grandmother, will work to diligently teach them the truth of God. We desire to give them the correct spiritual foundation with which to meet the world's challenges. Perhaps the most demanding of parenting behaviors, sacrifice, will be the hallmark of our parenting, as it is of our Heavenly Father. This sacrifice is not the kind that provides more toys, more lessons, more vacations, etc., but the kind of sacrifice that allows a child to be trained by the suffering of doing without extras or of having to work for them, or by experiencing promised consequences of foolish or rebellious behavior. The mother must suffer the sacrifice of temporarily not being regarded as a friend by the child, in order to reinforce behavior pleasing to God. Mothers courageous enough to engage in this sort of sacrifice aspire to see adult children who are productive contributors, not only to the world around them, but also to the kingdom of God.

Perhaps the most courage is required of Christian mothers when their children appear to reject all the efforts that have been made to lead them to choose Christian lives. No realistic discussion of being a mother can exclude this possibility. Just as the majority of God's chosen people rejected Jesus, the fulfillment of His promised plan for salvation, many children do reject the church as soon as they leave home. The variables in families and individuals which lead to this decision are as numerous as the people involved. In spite of our great love for our children, our youthful aspirations to be better at parenting than our own parents, our prayers, and our best efforts, there are no perfect parents, just as there are no perfect people. When our imperfections seem to lead to bad choices on the part of our children, we are humbled and can be tempted to lose our faith. When the children of our brothers and sisters in Christ make this tragic choice, the entire family is in need of the prayers and encouragement, rather than the judgment of the church family.

The parable of the Prodigal Son in Luke 15:11-32 contains valuable lessons for us to consider. The account is in the context of several accounts Jesus was sharing with his dinner partners who happened to be tax collectors and sinners. The common theme in the first ten verses of the chapter is the value to God of each individual. Jesus begins the story of this young man with his demand to be given his inheritance early, followed by his abrupt departure from the family. We notice, first of all, the father gave the son his request. He allowed the son his free will and gave him the wealth, in spite of knowing that the son was not ready for it and would waste it. We must remember, as much as we love the children God has given into our care, these young people are souls who belong to God and are not possessions under our control. They are not porcelain figurines, beautifully painted for the purpose of adorning a shelf in our homes, proclaiming our success to all the world. They are most valuable individuals, creations of God, whose love and adoration He desires, just as He does ours. They must be allowed to choose how they will live; He will allow them to make mistakes and even turn from Him, in the hope they will learn from their experiences, repent, and return in sincere obedience to Him.

In Luke 15:20, after the son has lost everything and in humility has decided to return to his home, we read before he even reached home, his father ran to meet him. The father never gave up on his son. He did not disown him in hatred, declaring him dead, and live the rest of his life as if the son did not exist. The father was waiting and watching for his return. There is no indication in this passage the father invited the son to bring his wild friends and partying life into the family home. Rather, when the son was ready to leave that life behind, the father welcomed him with open arms. In verses 22-24, as well as in verse 32, the father describes the celebration to be given to this returning son and says he had to rejoice because he was "lost and has been found." The value of each of us, including our rebellious children, to God is that we exist, not that we are obedient. We must have the same priority with our wandering children. We are not required to approve of their choice to sin, but we must be ready to forgive and accept them back when they choose to repent. Satan tells the teenage daughter her parents will "kill her" for getting pregnant, so she runs away or has an abortion. The greatest argument she can see for returning to God is when those parents, through their tears, reach for her and commit to help her with the consequences of her actions. The parents who show their rebellious son or daughter the agape love of 1 Corinthians 13:4-7 through the years, trying to meet with them regularly and include them in family gatherings, show the same kind of watchfulness as the father of the prodigal son.

As I have observed parents of young adults and am now a parent of adults, I have seen a common pitfall for some loving mothers is not being able to let go of their children. Sometimes this results in children not leaving home, and other times it manifests itself as a mother who becomes the go-to person for the children in every decision they make. There are a few biblical examples of controlling moms, and we will consider them here.

Sarai, Abraham's wife, was controlling before she even had children. Having grown impatient with God because His promise of a son had not yet been fulfilled, we read of her interference.

Courage as Mothers: Choose to Train Your Children

> Now Sarai, Abram's wife had borne him no children, and she had an Egyptian maid whose name was Hagar. So Sarai said to Abram, "Now behold, the LORD has prevented me from bearing children. Please go in to my maid; perhaps I will obtain children through her." And Abram listened to the voice of Sarai. After Abram had lived ten years in the land of Canaan, Abram's wife Sarai took Hagar the Egyptian, her maid, and gave her to her husband Abram as his wife. He went in to Hagar, and she conceived; and when she saw that she had conceived, her mistress was despised in her sight. And Sarai said to Abram, "May the wrong done me be upon you. I gave my maid into your arms, but when she saw that she had conceived, I was despised in her sight. May the LORD judge between you and me" (Genesis 16:1-5).

Another example of the controlling, interfering mom type is Rebekah, the wife of Isaac. Read her strategy to advance Jacob to the blessing of the eldest son.

> Rebekah was listening while Isaac spoke to his son Esau. So when Esau went to the field to hunt for game to bring home, Rebekah said to her son Jacob, "Behold, I heard your father speak to your brother Esau, saying, 'Bring me some game and prepare a savory dish for me, that I may eat, and bless you in the presence of the LORD before my death.' Now therefore, my son, listen to me as I command you. Go now to the flock and bring me two choice young goats from there, that I may prepare them as a savory dish for your father, such as he loves. Then you shall bring it to your father, that he may eat, so that he may bless you before his death." Jacob answered his mother Rebekah, "Behold, Esau my brother is a hairy man and I am a smooth man. Perhaps my father will feel me, then I will be as a deceiver in his sight, and I will bring upon myself a curse and not a blessing." But his mother said to him, "Your curse be on me, my son; only obey my voice, and go, get them for me." Then Rebekah took the best garments of Esau her elder son, which were with her in the house, and put them on Jacob her younger son. And she put the skins of the young goats on his hands, and the smooth part of his neck. She also gave the savory food and the bread, which she had made, to her son Jacob (Genesis 27:5-13, 15-17).

Deeper study into these two examples of moms who meddled where they had no right reveals the son of Hagar, Ishmael, became the father of the Arab people. To this day we know the Arabs and the Jews are in continual conflict. Sarai's rash behavior continues to have consequences today. The day the plot by Jacob and Rebekah was unveiled, Jacob had to flee for his life; Rebekah lost her favored, precious son. Esau's relationship with his parents was destroyed as he rebelled by taking a wife from the people of Ishmael. Jacob lived for decades in a foreign land because of his fear of his brother's retaliation. God used all of these circumstances to His will for good, but there can be no doubt that these mothers did great damage.

One example in the New Testament of a mother who could not let go of her sons is found in the Gospel of Matthew.

> Then the mother of the sons of Zebedee came to Jesus with her sons, bowing down and making a request of Him. And He said to her, "What do you wish?" She said to Him, "Command that in Your kingdom these two sons of mine may sit one on Your right and one on Your left." But Jesus answered, "You do not know what you are asking. Are you able to drink the cup that I am about to drink?" They said to Him, "We are able." He said to them, "My cup you shall drink; but to sit on My right and on My left, this is not Mine to give, but it is for those for whom it has been prepared by My Father" (Matthew 20: 20-23).

If any of these mothers had had the least idea of the consequences of their actions, how long and deep and devastating they were, would they have still interfered for the sake of the short term advancement of their sons?

It takes courage and faith in God to let go of our children when they have reached adulthood. We can listen to them and be a sounding board, but we must remember that they belong to God, and we must carefully guard against the natural tendency to interfere with His plans for them. There are no good examples in the Bible of mothers interfering in the decisions of their adult children. The courageous mother continues to pray and hope for her children always. She recognizes her children are gifts, a stewardship from a God who loves them even more than she does, and therefore intimately understands the pain she experiences when they face difficulties and pain in life. As her children become adults and she sees them react to life in faith and obedience to the Bible, she learns to trust even more in the love and faithfulness of God in all things.

CHAPTER NINE **Questions for Discussion**

1. Does relying on the Bible for the most important principles of parenting imply that we can learn nothing about the phases of children's growth from secular sources?
2. If you agree that marriage goes against the popular culture in the United States, do you believe young people are pressured not to have children in this country?
3. How can childless couples unable to adopt children work to help children grow up to be Christians?
4. What can the examples of Sarai, Rebekah, and the mother of James and John teach us about attempting to manipulate our children's futures?
5. How does meditating on God's parenting style with us help us to prioritize our activities with our children?

CHAPTER TEN

Courage in the Church (Part I): Choose to Love Your Brothers and Sisters

Are you old enough to remember the following words?

> "I love thy kingdom, Lord, the house of Thine abode. The church our blest Redeemer saved with His own precious blood. I love Thy church O God! Her walls before thee stand, dear as the apple of thine eye and graven on thy hand. For her my tears shall fall, for her my prayers ascend; to her my cares and toils be given, till toils and cares shall end. Beyond my highest joy I prize her heavenly ways, her sweet communion, solemn vows, her hymns of love and praise. Jesus, Thou Friend divine, Our Savior and Our King, Thy hand from every snare and foe, shall great deliverance bring. Sure as thy truth shall last, to Zion shall be given the brightest glories earth can yield, and brighter bliss of heaven."

In the year 1800, Timothy Dwight penned these words, which were joined with music written by Lowell Mason, to become the hymn, "I Love Thy Kingdom, Lord." I grew up singing this song, an encouragement to perceive the church as a precious group of people, brought together by the sacrificial blood of Jesus Christ. One hundred seventy-five years later, Lanny Wolfe crafted another hymn, "God's Family" which also expresses the simple, yet priceless love members of the church are to have for one another, the unsurpassed value of our association. The chorus of this beautiful song can bring tears to the eyes.

Courage in the Church (Part I): Choose to Love Your Brothers and Sisters

> "...And sometimes we laugh together, sometimes we cry; sometimes we share together, heart-aches and sighs; sometimes we dream together of how it will be when we all get to heaven, God's family."

As Christian women, eager to live in obedience to the authority of God, and to demonstrate biblical principles in our lives and homes, this chapter helps us consider how necessary it is for us to show courage within our church families. For just as Satan seeks to destroy our faith through our minds and homes, he is busy attempting to break down individual relationships and congregations. Statistics reveal that he is having great success in these areas.

> A case in point is that only half of American adults (53 percent) contend that their religious faith is very important in their life these days. That proportion has declined slowly but steadily over the last twenty years. A more convincing piece of evidence concerns the well-documented dismissal of faith by the under-thirty crowd. Most studies now show that roughly one-third of them have no connection to organized religion and that their distaste for organized religion is growing steadily....A growing number of adults now describe themselves as "spiritual but not religious," by which they mean they are open to and accepting of things related to faith and the supernatural but not inclined toward routines, traditions, doctrines, and faith systems. This newer view is especially in vogue among people born after 1980. Despite the expectations of a society that demands a tolerance of all points of view, it is difficult to mask the fact that the shift toward being spiritual but not religious is taking a toll on America's devotion to God and its long-standing connection to Christianity.[1]

In God's Word we can find wisdom and power to overcome these successful attacks. Our courage can lift up members whose faith is weak, our humility and honesty borne of agape love can strengthen bonds in God's family, and our examples of these qualities can educate and empower young women who are members of today's churches. For one day when we are gone, and they remain, they will need to do the same.

The book of Acts chronicles the history of the establishment of New Testament churches. In the epistles of Paul, James, Peter, and John we learn about the relationships between the individuals in those congregations. We do not have to read far in these books to see that the problems that plague our relationships today are nothing new! Division, pride, racism, hypocrisy, gossip, grudge-bearing, all these causes of chaos and discouragement in the body are universal problems in the church. They have been around from the beginning of time. Jesus made the perfect sacrifice for our souls and welcomes us into His kingdom through obedience to His Word. But we are still human beings, so the church will always be full of struggle. We are the family of God, but just as we understand there are no perfect human families, we must begin considering this topic by accepting the axiom that there are no perfect church families. As we learn and put into practice the skills needed to have healthy fellowship in our congregations, we get a glimpse of the love God has for us. Jesus prayed for the church to come the night before His crucifixion, saying,

> "I do not ask on behalf of these alone, but for those also who believe in Me through their word; that they may all be one; even as You, Father, are in Me and I in You, that they also may be in Us, so that the world may believe that You sent Me" (John 17:20-21).

Before we look at specific verses about how to treat one another in the church, I believe there is an example from the writings of Paul. How did he choose to treat the members of churches to which he wrote? Paul prayed with thanksgiving for his brethren. Consider the similarities of the following verses:

- "First, I thank my God through Jesus Christ for you all, because your faith is being proclaimed throughout the whole world" (Romans 1:8).

- "I thank my God always concerning you for the grace of God which was given you in Christ Jesus" (1 Corinthians 1:4).
- "For this reason I too, having heard of the faith in the Lord Jesus which exists among you and your love for all the saints, do not cease giving thanks for you, while making mention of you in my prayers" (Ephesians 1:15-16).
- "I thank my God in all my remembrance of you" (Philippians 1:3).
- "We give thanks to God, the Father of our Lord Jesus Christ, praying always for you" (Colossians 1:3).
- "We give thanks to God always for all of you, making mention of you in our prayers" (1 Thessalonians 1:2).
- "Therefore, we ourselves speak proudly of you among the churches of God for your perseverance and faith in the midst of all your persecutions and afflictions which you endure" (2 Thessalonians 1:4).
- "I thank God, whom I serve with a clear conscience the way my forefathers did, as I constantly remember you in my prayers night and day" (2 Timothy 1:3).
- "I thank my God always, making mention of you in my prayers" (Philemon 1:4).

In each of these epistles, Paul relayed to the congregations his ongoing thanksgiving to God for them. His thankfulness for the existence of these brethren in each of these regions was not conditional upon them being mature brethren. As parents, our love for our children co-exists with our earnest desire to help them mature into Christians pleasing to God. We understand that expressing our love to them is important in encouraging them on the right paths. Paul understood this with the churches to which he wrote. They had some serious problems, and he did not shrink from correction, but neither did he shrink from expressing to all of them his love and proving that by praying for them.

We have studied in detail the concept of prayer and considered the power of God to answer prayer. We can learn from these passages one courageous thing we can do as members of congregations is to remember the brethren individually and collectively in our personal prayers. If we are involved in difficulties with brothers or sisters, going to God in prayer about the situation is the wisest course of action in seeking a solution. Developing the habit of praying with thanksgiving for our congregations can help us treasure them more, and doing so in front of our children passes on that sense that the church is special.

James wrote to a broad audience, "To the twelve tribes who are dispersed abroad" in 1:1. He referred to them several times in his epistle as "My brethren." Peter and John both used the term "Beloved," a term embracing their readers as well or dearly loved with the agape love of the Bible, that love which seeks the highest or eternal good of the one loved. John also referred to the church as a "Chosen Lady" and to the members as his "Little Children." These terms of endearment go beyond the superficial sentimentality of a social club. They reflect an intimacy separate from the world. As we read the books in which these terms of endearment are found, we observe that Peter and John expressed this care for the brethren in spite of their problems and lack of maturity. In the same way, it is appropriate for us to show high regard for the imperfect people with whom we attend church.

Observations of congregations from my childhood to the present cause me to believe a great stumbling block to real growth in congregations is a universal difficulty to resolve conflicts between members. I have never met a Christian for whom conflict resolution was an easy, pleasant experience. I have met Christians who have struggled with whether or not to leave the church because of how a conflict in which they were involved was handled. I have heard stories of people who left the church after a conflict. Because as adults we have difficulty with this, we are not teaching our young people how to handle conflict with fellow Christian young people. Their youth groups are plagued with the same dramas as their junior high and high school classes. We are given clear directions in scripture, as well as biblical examples of conflict resolution between Christians. In spite of these Scriptures, any honest person will admit they have difficulty with this. Those like me who struggle with anger have had many more mistakes than successes in getting through conflicts with brothers and sisters in the church. Let us review some of what the New Testament reveals about how to treat one another, especially in the area of conflicts.

Improving our ability to resolve conflicts with brothers and sisters in Christ begins with how we think about ourselves. As Jesus teaches about the greatest commandments, He says,

> "The second is like it, 'You shall love your neighbor as yourself'" (Matthew 22:39).

As Paul instructs husbands in loving their wives in Ephesians, he incidentally discusses legitimate self-love.

> "He who loves his wife loves himself; for no one ever hated his own flesh, but nourishes and cherishes it, just as Christ also does the church" (Ephesians 5:28-29).

God expects that we will love ourselves and does not require us to set that aside. However, in learning how to imitate Christ we learn to expand self-love to include others.

> Do nothing from selfishness or empty conceit, but with humility of mind regard one another as more important than yourselves; do not merely look out for your own personal interests, but also for the interests of others. Have this attitude in yourselves which was also in Christ Jesus, who, although He existed in the form of God, did not regard equality with God a thing to be grasped, but emptied Himself, taking the form of a bond-servant, and being made in the likeness of men. Being found in appearance as a man, He humbled Himself by becoming obedient to the point of death, even death on a cross. (Philippians 2:3-8)

In this familiar set of verses we are reminded that Jesus was fully aware of His rank as God. But something that is so important to humans was unimportant to Him; he laid that rank down. He humbled Himself and obeyed His father. Paul urges us, his readers, to cultivate humility that allows us to place other people's welfare above our own. In the following passage we see an intimate example of Jesus' regard and sacrifice.

> Now before the Feast of the Passover, Jesus knowing that His hour had come that He would depart out of this world to the Father, having loved His own who were in the world, He loved them to the end. During supper, the devil having already put into the heart of Judas Iscariot, the son of Simon, to betray Him, Jesus, knowing that the Father had given all things into His hands, and that He had come forth from God and was going back to God, got up from supper, and laid aside His garments; and taking a towel, He girded Himself. Then He poured water into the basin, and began to wash the disciples' feet and to wipe them with the towel with which He was girded (John 13:1-5).

At this event, this last dinner with his disciples, Jesus humbled Himself to the level of the lowest servant so that He could illustrate for them how they ought to behave toward one another. Consider His words to them,

> "...Do you know what I have done to you? You call Me Teacher and Lord; and you are right, for so I am. If I then, the Lord and the Teacher, washed your feet, you also ought to wash one another's feet. For I gave you an example that you also should do as I did to you" (John 13:12-15).

Once again, notice that Jesus did not ignore His position as Teacher and Lord. He did not, however, allow that position to keep Him from sacrificing His dignity in this instance to teach them about humbling themselves.

There is an unusual statement in verse two of our reading. In John's set-up of the scene in the upper room, he notes that Judas Iscariot had already become the tool of the devil in his heart, determining to betray Jesus. As John lists all of the things Jesus "knew" at the beginning of this last evening with His disciples, this terrible decision by Judas is in the midst of the list. John writes that Jesus let his dear friends know he knew of this betrayal that would lead to His death.

> "When Jesus had said this, He became troubled in spirit, and testified and said, 'Truly, truly, I say to you, that one of you will betray Me'" (John 13:21).

Humbling ourselves and sacrificing our time, our energy, our emotions, and risking mistakes in new endeavors for our brothers and sisters in Christ is a difficult concept. When we consider what Christ has done for us, most of us can work ourselves up to it if we see a great need. However, if we are hurt or betrayed by someone for whom we are sacrificing, our first instinct is to bail out of whatever it is to which we have committed. The shock of hurt or betrayal we feel after a critical dressing down by a brother or sister can turn us completely off from risking any future involvement in things like Bible class teaching or serving in the worship. I have seen young adult members withdraw almost completely within themselves and never develop their talents because an older member corrected them in what they thought was an unloving manner. It is important for us to look to Scripture for Jesus' example on dealing with betrayal, because He knew the betrayal was coming, as surely as He knew He would go through with the sacrifice anyway. Jesus maintained His spiritual focus, understanding that hurt, betrayal, and evil were tools of Satan, not the human involved.

How many of our conflicts would be more easily diffused if we understood that Satan was behind the mischief between us? If you have been hurt by members and discouraged from risking new service to the Lord, consider the following Scriptures:

> "A disciple is not above his teacher, nor a slave above his master. It is enough for the disciple that he become like his teacher, and

the slave like his master. If they have called the head of the house Beelzebul, how much more will they malign the members of his household!" (Matthew 10:24-25)

"Then they will deliver you to tribulation, and will kill you, and you will be hated by all nations because of My name. At that time many will fall away and will betray one another and hate one another. Many false prophets will arise and will mislead many. Because lawlessness is increased, most people's love will grow cold. But the one who endures to the end, he will be saved" (Matthew 24:9-13).

Satan uses people, especially Christians when he can get them, to discourage us. This is a hard thing for us to accept, but it is true. Finally, meditate on this Scripture:

For you have been called for this purpose, since Christ also suffered for you, leaving you an example for you to follow in His steps, WHO COMMITTED NO SIN, NOR WAS ANY DECEIT FOUND IN HIS MOUTH; and while being reviled, He did not revile in return; while suffering, He uttered no threats, but kept entrusting Himself to Him who judges righteously; and He Himself bore our sins in His body on the cross, so that we might die to sin and live to righteousness; for by His wounds you were healed (1 Peter 2:21-24).

We have so far covered actions and attitudes that can give us courage to cherish the congregations of which we are members. We have reviewed the examples of Paul, James, Peter, and John in making a habit of thankful prayer for the Christians, even though they were full of flaws. We have recognized that as human beings we are equipped with a natural love for ourselves that helps us protect and nourish ourselves. We have also been reminded of the example of our Savior, who expanded that self-love to include the human race. We have been reminded that His ultimate sacrifice was rewarded with betrayal and hatred by the majority of mankind. We have learned from His example of trust in His Father that we can trust God to comfort and reward us as we face betrayal and hurt in trying to do what is right. We now understand that conflict among members of the body of Christ is as inevitable as it is in our human families. We can see that such conflict and the pain that comes with it are not reasons to leave the church, because Christ faced much worse and did not leave the cross.

There are some familiar passages dealing with conflict resolution from which most of us can benefit by reviewing often, and we will review those now. In our ladies' class we have been blessed by studying from Jane McWhorter's book, *Now I Can Fly* (Publishing Designs) and is available from 21st Century Christian Bookstore. Her honest, practical, biblical lessons are challenging and valuable. In her chapter, "Forgive as Commanded" she makes the important point that as Christians it is our responsibility to take initiative to heal relationships that are damaged, whether we are the one who has been wronged or the ones who has done the wrong.[2]

> "If your brother sins, go and show him his fault in private; if he listens to you, you have won your brother" (Matthew 18:15).

> "Therefore if you are presenting your offering at the altar, and there remember that your brother has something against you, leave your offering there before the altar and go; first be reconciled to your brother, and then come and present your offering" (Matthew 5:23-24).

As Jesus was expanding on the true intent of the Ten Commandments during what we call the Sermon on the Mount, He includes these instructions on rebuilding broken relationships in the section on the command against murder. If as sisters we were to be courageous enough to follow these directions of Jesus literally, our attendance at services might be occasionally replaced with quiet meetings attempting to solve problems. Our services would be more joyful if the members in attendance worshiped without resentment and with peace, everyone feeling safe and included in the family. If we gave up holding grudges and engaging in conversations about nothing to cover our feelings, but instead:

> Therefore, laying aside falsehood, SPEAK TRUTH EACH ONE of you WITH HIS NEIGHBOR, for we are members of one another. BE ANGRY AND yet DO NOT SIN; do not let the sun go down on your anger, and do not give the devil an opportunity (Ephesians 4:25-27).

Wouldn't we be healthier physically, without unexplained headaches, depression, anxiety, stomach, or back problems? And if Christians became known in our cultures as people who had positive, loving relationships with those around them, how much brighter would our light shine in this dark world? [2]

Paul exhorted the Colossian Christians,

> So, as those who have been chosen of God, holy and beloved, put on a heart of compassion, kindness, humility, gentleness and patience; bearing with one another, and forgiving each other, whoever has a complaint against anyone; just as the Lord forgave you, so also should you. Beyond all these things put on love, which is the perfect bond of unity (Colossians 3:12-14).

In our congregations there can be a wide variety of maturity levels. My husband and I have been attending the same congregation for more than 30 years. When we first started going, I was still in my teenage years, having married at 18. Over the decades of my life, many members have had hearts of compassion for me, teaching me in kindness, humility, gentleness, and patience. They have had to bear with me as they waited for the light of maturity to come on in my head and life in many respects. I have benefitted from much forgiveness.

As I have passed into middle age, I find myself needing to be on the giving end of these things. Prayer for others has become important as I pray that they will seek God's will and learn from Him how to correct poor choices they make. Because of the experiences in my life, I have had some practice in discerning right from wrong and in looking ahead to consequences of choices. This may cause me to question the choices of younger sisters at times. But there is a difference in expressing words of caution to someone regarding choices they make and pronouncing eternal condemnation on them for a sin. I want to remember to temper my concern for others with a recognition that each is a precious soul. Paul, while discussing how we conduct our relationships with Christians whose consciences are different than ours, instructed,

"Do not destroy with your food him for whom Christ died" (Romans 14:15).

In our congregation we have recently had several lessons from Ron White about these matters and they have been reminders worth sharing. Whether it is food or holidays or my style of correction, I must remember that the person with whom I interact is as valuable to Christ as I am. Our conflicts will be more easily solved if we allow our personalities to conform to the following Scripture: "Let your gentle spirit be known to all men" (Philippians 4:5).[3]

In Philippians 4:2 we read of two very human, very precious Christian sisters, Euodia and Syntyche, who were struggling in their relationship. Not long ago I was privileged in to be in a Bible class on Philippians, where one of the preachers discussed his belief that the entire book was written for the two women mentioned in that verse.[4] How would we react to having our name in the Bible because we were having a long-standing fight with a Christian sister? But I find the next verse of that chapter comforting. Paul writes:

Indeed, true companion, I ask you also to help these women who have shared my struggle in the cause of the gospel, together with Clement also and the rest of my fellow workers, whose names are in the book of life (Philippians 4:3).

Paul held out hope that these women could resolve their differences, reconcile their relationship, and that their names remained in the book of life. We know that Jesus said regarding conflicts:

> "For if you forgive others for their transgressions, your heavenly Father will also forgive you. But if you do not forgive others, then your Father will not forgive your transgressions" (Matthew 6:14-15).

Whether the whole book of Philippians was truly written to address the trouble between these two women or not, we understand that resolving conflicts between ourselves and brothers and sisters in Christ, indeed with anyone, is critical to our salvation. Most of us know from experience that it is difficult and requires humility, true agape love, and most of all courage to follow this command. I pray that we will all courageously choose to treasure our brothers and sisters in Christ and keep our relationships in our church families healthy, that the world may know us by our love.

CHAPTER TEN **Questions for Discussion**

1. How do Jesus' commands for conflict resolution differ from our impulses as humans?
2. Discuss ways we can prepare ourselves to accept correction graciously.
3. Discuss ways we can prepare ourselves to initiate conversations about conflict graciously.
4. If you have had an experience with conflict resolution that went according to Scripture, please share it with the group.
5. Discuss methods of passing on this wisdom to teenage girls and younger women.
6. Do you believe if we demonstrate scriptural attitudes and actions regarding conflict resolution in our church families, we can retain more of our young people, reversing the statistics quoted at the beginning of the chapter?

References

1. Barna, George and Barton, David 2014. U-turn, Restoring America to the Strength of its Roots, pg. 26. Published by FrontLine Charisma Media/Charisma House Book Group, Lake Mary, Florida, United States.
2. McWhorter, Jane, 2011. Now I can fly, Living Victoriously, pgs. 111-121. Published by Publishing Designs Inc., Huntsville, Alabama, United States.
3. Ron White, minister, Wasatch church of Christ, lessons given in December 2014 regarding matters of opinion between Christians.
4. Tony Pyrtle, member of Logan church of Christ, lesson given at 2014 Utah Labor Day Lectureship, "Balanced Relationships; Your Liberty, My Rights."

CHAPTER 11

Courage in the Church (Part 2): Choose to Embrace Your Place

As we revisit Paul's final farewell with the elders to the church of Ephesus, he said,

> "Be on your guard for yourselves and for all the flock, among which the Holy Spirit has made you overseers, to shepherd the church of God which He purchased with His own blood. I know that after my departure savage wolves will come in among you, not sparing the flock; and from among your own selves men will arise, speaking perverse things, to draw away the disciples after them" (Acts 20:28-30).

In Revelation 2:1-7 we read from John the warning given to the Ephesian church, indicating that they had indeed fallen from the healthy state they were in when Paul was with them.

Paul also exhorted Timothy in his second letter to study the truths he had been taught, and we commonly take that passage in 2 Timothy 2:15 for ourselves as encouragement that we should be able to handle the Word of Truth accurately. The apostle Peter addressed his first letter "To those who reside as aliens, scattered throughout Pontus, Galatia, Cappadocia, Asia, and Bithynia" (1 Peter 1:1). One of his instructions was as follows:

> ...but sanctify Christ as Lord in your hearts, always being ready to make a defense to everyone who asks you to give an account for the hope that is in you, yet with gentleness and reverence (1 Peter 3:15).

Courage in the Church (Part 2): Choose to Embrace Your Place

An important duty of all Christians is to make certain the things we are being taught in lessons and sermons, and the things we teach to others, are true to the Bible. We are surrounded by examples of false teaching in the world, but we must also be alert to the attempts Satan makes to bring false teaching into the Lord's church. In this chapter it is my goal to make you aware of research I have done into a movement that is suddenly coming out of the shadows where it has hidden for generations. It is not a new doctrine and it is one that the Word of God addresses. It is important for women to understand these things because the woman's role in the assembly and organization of the church is the target of this false teaching. It is not my intention in this one chapter to quarrel angrily with the authors of articles, books, or participants in the videos that I have researched. Rather, it is my hope that readers who have not had time to investigate these things on their own will be encouraged to make time to study the Scriptures provided and increase their awareness of what is being taught in their congregations, standing in humble and loving opposition to any of the error that might creep into the teachings they hear as this movement attempts to spread. The following Scriptures from Paul are my cautions as I begin to share this information:

> But the goal of our instruction is love from a pure heart and a good conscience and a sincere faith (1 Timothy 1:5).

> The Lord's bond-servant must not be quarrelsome, but be kind to all, able to teach, patient when wronged, with gentleness correcting those who are in opposition, if perhaps God may grant them repentance leading to the knowledge of the truth, and they may come to their senses and escape from the snare of the devil, having been held captive by him to do his will (2 Timothy 2:24-26).

The teachings of those who would place women in leadership positions in the formal assembly and organizations of the church are incremental in nature and begin with their perception of the Lord's church as tied to human history. Rather than identifying with the Lord's church as established on the Day of Pentecost shortly after Christ's resurrection in fulfillment of prophecy as related by Luke in Acts 2, authors of books embracing this and other false doctrines define the churches of Christ as outgrowths of the Restoration movement in the United States. They revere Alexander Campbell and Barton W. Stone as church fathers and claim the church of Christ as their religious heritage.[1] In doing this they not only ignore historical evidence of churches of Christ existing internationally previous to its arrival in our country; these theologians and professors instruct their naïve readers to conceptualize the church as equal with denominations. They set aside warnings such as,

- But even if we, or an angel from heaven, should preach to you a gospel contrary to what we have preached to you, he is to be accursed! (Galatians 1:8)
- Jesus Christ is the same yesterday and today and forever (Hebrews 13:8).

These are but two verses that express the supremacy and permanence of the teachings of the New Testament.

These philosophers and preachers instead offer a perspective on the Bible that wraps itself in human reason. Their agenda requires that Christians be retrained from perceiving the Bible as the once-given-all-sufficient Word of God to a love letter or set of guidelines that must be reviewed by each generation with eyes that take in to account the prevailing cultural and societal norms. In advocating this, they ignore clear teachings such as:

> And do not be conformed to this world, but be transformed by the renewing of your mind, so that you may prove what the will of God is, that which is good and acceptable and perfect (Romans 12:2).

Courage in the Church (Part 2): Choose to Embrace Your Place

In this verse, Paul tells the ordinary Roman Christians that not only were they capable of understanding God's will without theological degrees, they were commanded to be so immersed in the Word of God that they would be transformed, be different from the world around them because of their understanding. Paul's intention was clearly that the Word of God would change the Christians, not the other way around. Peter expanded on Paul's sentiment in the following passage of his second epistle,

> Grace and peace be multiplied to you in the knowledge of God and of Jesus our Lord; seeing that His divine power has granted to us everything pertaining to life and godliness, through the true knowledge of Him who called us by His own glory and excellence. For by these He has granted to us His precious and magnificent promises, so that by them you may become partakers of the divine nature, having escaped the corruption that is in the world by lust. Now for this very reason also, applying all diligence, in your faith supply moral excellence, and in your moral excellence, knowledge, and in your knowledge, self-control, and in your self-control, perseverance, and in your perseverance, godliness, and in your godliness, brotherly kindness, and in your brotherly kindness, love. For if these qualities are yours and are increasing, they render you neither useless nor unfruitful in the true knowledge of our Lord Jesus Christ. For he who lacks these qualities is blind or short-sighted, having forgotten his purification from his former sins. Therefore, brethren, be all the more diligent to make certain about His calling and choosing you; for as long as you practice these things, you will never stumble (2 Peter 1:2-10).

Instead of being content with having "everything pertaining to life and godliness" and the true gospel, peddlers of false doctrine flatter their hearers into believing that because of their advanced education and sociological understanding of today's culture, they have the authority to re-interpret the Scriptures. The implication of this dogma is almost evolutionary; that the Christians of all the centuries previous to our own understood the teachings of the Bible in only primitive ways, specifically teachings regarding women's roles. Though they claim to revere what they refer to as their religious heritage, it is only in the sense of a dear fairy tale that they have now outgrown and wish to set aside.

This notion of a gospel that changes with the times based upon the whims of highly educated religious experts is a familiar one in my home state of Utah, as is another pillar of all innovations of religious doctrine, that of pleasant emotions. The majority of Utahans still claim to be members of the Church of Jesus Christ of Latter-Day Saints. When a prospective convert is studying with the missionaries here or abroad, the major foundation upon which they are asked to base their choice to join the church is called the "burning in the bosom." People studying with missionaries and young members take a vow that they will study no material that is contradictory to what they are being taught, so that the peaceful feelings in their hearts will not be disturbed. Faithful believers in this religion make all major decisions based upon whether or not the choice will bring them happiness and a sense of peace. Teachings of the newest apostles and the current Prophet always take precedence over the old teachings, and so there have been many major changes in the doctrines of the church. The Bible is said to be part of their scriptures only to the degree that it is translated correctly, and correct translation is determined by the feelings of the church leaders. Members are taught that when the Prophet in Salt Lake City has made a decree on a matter, the thinking has been done, so they turn off otherwise intelligent minds and blindly follow the experts. They add children to their families based upon feelings and dreams. The extreme result of this emotionally based church leadership is sexual predators who disguise themselves as modern-day prophets with multiple wives, some of whom are as young as 13.

The same supremacy of emotions in spirituality permeates the congregations of the Lord's body where these false teachings

Courage in the Church (Part 2): Choose to Embrace Your Place

about women's roles in the church are being accepted. Recently, a Vimeo video was released, "Meet Lauren King, Preaching Intern at the 4th avenue church of Christ." This young woman stated in her presentation,

> "A lot of the ways that I perceive the Lord's voice is through having peace when I walk through open doors. If I have an unpeaceful heart then that's not really where I'm supposed to be. But if I'm in a place where I have peace about where I'm going, then that's the Lord telling me yes."
> (The choice of words is a direct quote.)[5]

She offered no scriptural basis for what she was doing, only her feelings. In this video also was the male preacher for the congregation, Patrick Mead. Consider the remarks he made on this video:

> "For a long time we have talked about the way we value women here, and the way we believe Scripture values women. I do not believe that Paul in two verses, two passages was trying to undo the rest of Scripture. I think he was addressing a temporary issue in Corinth and Ephesus and I think that if we know our history, we can see what it was. He was not making rules for everywhere and every time, or we would not be allowing widows to be fed if they were a certain age, and we would not be allowing women to have jewelry on, these were temporary things for temporary times. What the Bible does is it tells me about Jesus. And I don't read Jesus through Paul, I read Paul through Jesus. And I think churches of Christ are getting this, that **WE NO LONGER READ ALL OF THE BIBLE AS EQUAL**, but rather we come to Jesus. The Old Law and the Prophets brought us to Him. The transfiguration, listen to Him. Now everything Paul said, he was a fellow student with us. Let's read it through Jesus."[5]

What was recorded in this video, the first sermon by this young woman in a church service, was the culmination of a process of changes in the minds and the hearts of the members. The woman who serves as the Minister of Administration in the congregation said the following on the video,

"It's a blessing to have Lauren here. We're a church that embraces a lot of diversity. We want to be a body of unity and embrace differences, and sometimes we don't walk that out very comfortably, we stagger and stumble and trip over ourselves in that. But it's just that part of being open to change; if that is what Jesus is calling us to do, we're ready to do it. But it's a process, but our family is learning how to do it better."[5]

Dear sisters, there is indeed a process here, and we can learn it, we can be on the look-out for it, we can respond to it to preserve the truth in our congregations. Just as the most meaningful support for the biblical submission of women to their husbands comes from the examples of the submissive wives in our congregations, the most meaningful preservation of our congregations against this false doctrine of women stepping outside of their role in the assembly will come from women.

As the preacher pointed out in the video, there had been a lot of discussion in their congregation about how the Bible values women. These discussions are happening in many congregations as feminist philosophies are accepted by Christians. The cause of feminism in America and throughout the Western world is one of the greatest examples of political correctness in society. This book has already covered the degrading effect this has had on men and boys and how the very future of our nation is threatened. These things spill over in to church life. In her book, *A Woman Called, Piecing Together the Ministry Puzzle*, Sara Gaston Barton describes growing up participating in the church of Christ "Heritage." As a member, she felt left out and treated as second class because she was barred from leading in the assembly. She grew to adulthood and achieved her degrees: a BA in English from Harding University and a Masters of Spiritual Formation and Leadership from Spring Arbor University. She first worked in overseas evangelism and then became a campus minister at Rochester College. She recounts the story of being shunned when she tried to preach in the churches of Christ in contrast to the

Courage in the Church (Part 2): Choose to Embrace Your Place

peace she felt when she preached in the Community church. This inner peace has guided her throughout her career. She believes because the teachings of the Bible must be reviewed and adapted to fit every generation, what she is doing is right because of the peace and satisfaction she gains from it.[1]

This process of changing hearts and minds in congregations to accept this false doctrine seems to commonly begin with getting the women to feel they have not been adequately valued in congregations where they are not permitted to take leading roles in the formal worship assembly. Just as Satan succeeded in causing Eve to feel God was keeping wonderful knowledge from her, naïve women feel they are being excluded from something unique by not preaching. They may be Bible class teachers, but teaching babies and children, even teaching ladies' classes, is devalued by those for whom the only real value is in teaching men. The women may be church secretaries, work with visiting the elderly, assist in organizing potlucks, and perform independent community service, but the holy grail of using the gifts they have received from God to those who promote this doctrine is taking the speaking roles in one or more of the formal assemblies of the church each week. The incremental nature of this change may take the subtle forms of first having the women assist in serving the communion, then they begin to lead prayers in the service, because women are so much better at leading beautiful prayers than the men. Finally, the women begin to teach the adult Bible classes, rather than just make comments in them. At last, a young woman who is an intern at a Christian university is brought in to fulfill her requirement for her academic degree, that degree giving her the credentials and authority to be a minister of the Lord's church, rather than biblical teaching. The rationale for placing women in each of these roles is that they have talents that ought to be used more fully.[5]

As the Minister of Administration honestly pointed out, this process is a messy one. Even the young intern pointed out in her "sermon" that not all of the members had chosen to attend the service where the young woman was preaching. Not all of the members were in favor of this change, but it was being made over their objections. She called for spiritual unity in the congregation, even alluding to Ephesians 4:3 that urges maintaining the unity of the spirit in the bond of peace. However, her definition of unity, as well as Patrick Mead's and all who hold to this doctrine, is that the backward members of the congregations capitulate to the greater understanding of the academically trained men and women and support this innovation in the churches of Christ.[5]

At the 1990 Freed-Hardeman Preacher's Forum, there was a discussion of the women's role in the church. Robert M. Randolph was one of the two preachers in the discussion in favor of women preaching and being elders in the church.[6] His argumentative article, "Why Women Should Be Preaching in the Churches of Christ" that appeared in the Pepperdine periodical, Leaven in 2003 expresses condescension and contempt for Christians who oppose his stance. Since he was a man of science who worked for a time for MIT, it was with great surprise that I read the emotionally-based arguments in this article. Secular standards for professionalism in scientific fields normally preclude the attitudes displayed.[3] It is important, in an effort to honestly represent the intentions of this man who has been a pillar in the movement to move women into leadership roles in the assembly of the church for me to share his writing in detail. His first argument is that the women of Jesus' day who followed Him and assisted His ministry held more authority than the women of today's congregations:

> "Phoebe (Romans 16) and Priscilla (Acts 18, Romans 16) are models of feminine participation in the early church. Debate may continue on the nature of their roles, but what is clear is that they had significant public exposure that would be unusual in many of our more traditional communities of faith today."[3]

Although he offers non-specific Scripture references where the women's names were mentioned, Mr. Randolph offers no specific examples to defend this assertion. Secondly, he attempts to build a case that "a church dominated by men only will find itself a source of scandal." He believes that when Paul was speaking about order in the church, he was only discussing a limited cultural context, and his answer to that is to declare,

> "...today we will be better served when it is known that in the community formed by Christ, women are valued, heard, and respected. Pulpits filled by men, and worship services led solely by men give precisely the opposite message."[3]

Again we see the words, *"valued, heard,* and *respected"* like a set of code words that should make us perk up our ears, and again the assumption is implicit that the only service of value in the churches is the formal assembly, negating all the value in other gatherings and contexts. Children and women are by exclusion degraded to second class by this assertion.[3]

As the article progresses, the author assigns childish, emotional motives to those who oppose his viewpoint, without any attempt to address their objections from Scripture. First of all he attacks with the assumption that men who oppose women in the pulpits feel their good old boys' club threatened:

> "But there are those who find it hard to imagine a woman as a minister. A friend recently chided me by suggesting that, in his congregation, if women preached there would soon be no men left attending or working. He is a good minister with a commitment to the proclamation of the gospel, but he feels threatened."[3]

Again, he declares,

> "It is my judgment that the 'something else' is that we have been conformed to a culture that is patriarchal and that gives men special privileges and roles... The Churches of Christ are essentially a 'men only' club that keeps women on the outside, in

part because we do not know any better, but more importantly because we are afraid. We are afraid to change a tradition that has given voice to women in secondary and manipulative ways. Stories abound of men who were dependent on their wives' social and intellectual talents leading in the church behind the veil of male leadership."[3]

Once the author has completed his indictment of male and female Christians in general, he moves on to specifically attack the concept of God held by Christians who do not agree with his judgments.

"Those who travel this road are also afraid of a God who struck down Nadab and Abihu because they offered strange fire. (No Scripture reference given.) They have institutionalized the fear of making mistakes. They consciously choose to put front and center a God who punishes capriciously. (Again, there is no Scripture reference to support the assertion that God has ever punished capriciously.) They could speak of the God who is the waiting father who kills the fatted calf when the prodigal returns home, the God who is the forgiving husband to the apostate nation of Israel…We are known by our choices, and when out of our fear we choose to silence half or more of our churches (women), then either we have not taken our Bibles seriously, or we are protecting something that benefits us." (Parentheses mine.)[3]

In seriously reading the allegations leveled at all Christians who disagree with this author, there are a couple of items worthy of notice in this text. First of all, the father of the prodigal son welcomed him home after he realized he was doing wrong, chose to repent, humbled himself, and returned home. There is no comparable scale offered in the article for what might cause the advocates of this doctrine to perform the same acts. Also, in the case of Israel, although God did accept them back every time they returned to Him, eventually, in AD 70, after multiple warnings, God brought about the complete destruction of that nation. Once Christ died and was raised and the church was established in Acts 2, the chosen people of God were those who heard the gospel and obeyed it. Israel's physical inheritance was lost because of their disobedience.[3]

There are a few Scriptures we must consider as we prepare ourselves to reject the insidious process of this attack by Satan on the body of Christ. We must be armed with the Word of God and honor our Lord as the final authority on the church.

> He is also the head of the body, the church; and He is the beginning, the firstborn from the dead, so that He Himself will come to have first place in everything (Colossians 1:18).

> To the woman He said, "I will greatly multiply your pain in childbirth, in pain you will bring forth children yet your desire will be for your husband, and he will rule over you" (Genesis 3:16).

We are familiar with the curse that God declared after Eve and Adam disobeyed Him, and this is where we begin to consider the place of women. Paul reiterated the order of authority between God and Man and Woman. Inspired by the Holy Spirit he wrote,

> But I want you to understand that Christ is the head of every man, and the man is the head of a woman, and God is the head of Christ (1 Corinthians 11:3).

Our erring brethren also begin their scriptural consideration in Genesis; however, they believe that once Jesus came, that order was nullified. The next Scripture they consider is in Galatians. Indeed this is the cornerstone of their entire doctrine.

> For you are all sons of God through faith in Christ Jesus. For all of you who were baptized into Christ have clothed yourselves with Christ. There is neither Jew nor Greek, there is neither slave nor free man, there is neither male nor female; for you are all one in Christ Jesus (Galatians 3:26-28).

They interpret this passage to mean that male and female genders are eliminated in Christ.

I am compelled to remind the reader that one of the proponents of this doctrine, in the video alluded to in this chapter, stated that Paul's teachings are not considered by him or his compatriots as being as important as Jesus' teachings, yet they are willing to base their entire movement for putting women in pulpits, as well as elderships, upon the phrase he wrote, "there is neither male nor female." So, like the members of the LDS church, these church leaders will decide which of Paul's teachings are important and which are not because it gives them warm feelings of honoring women to do so! And because they have decided this in their human wisdom, the ordinary Christian, like the ordinary Mormon, is to believe that "the thinking has been done." Sisters, I urge you to reject this.

Let us look at some of the Scriptures of Paul these innovating, erring brethren have been convinced by Satan to discard as not important. Let us begin with his letter to the troubled Corinthian church. The verse alluded to in 1 Corinthians 11 is at the beginning of a context, which those who have punctuated our Bibles have divided in to three chapters. This was done first by Cardinal Carl in A.D. 1236 and again by Robert Stephens in 1551, according to Halley's Bible Handbook. Toward the end of Paul's discussion about the formal assembly of the churches, he wrote,

> For God is not a God of confusion but of peace. As in all the churches of the saints, the women should keep silent in the churches. For they are not permitted to speak, but should be in submission as the Law also says (1 Corinthians 14:33-34, English Standard Version).[7]

Some versions of the Bible choose to separate verses 33 and 34 of that chapter so that the phrase "As in all the churches of the saints" is at the end of verse 33, rather than added to verse 34. One of the reasons this passage can be confusing is because of varying choices of the English punctuation added by various versions of the Bible. I researched the Bible Gateway website studying for this lesson and found that out of more than twenty versions and paraphrases of the Bible available on that website, thirteen of them had the punctuation arranged as the English Standard Version I have quoted above. This choice of punctuation makes it clear that it was Paul's universal teaching that the men were to lead the formal assemblies of the churches.[4]

A question may arise about the phrase "as the law also says" at the end of verse 34. This refers to citations in Exodus 24:1 and Numbers 18. In these two contexts God assigns Aaron and his sons as the Priests to serve in leading worship. Paul, who was teaching Christians after the church had been established, taught that the same order of authority present in Genesis 3:16 ought to be observed in the churches of the Lord, that the men were to lead. Reading on in 1 Corinthians 14:

> "If they desire to learn anything, let them ask their own husbands at home; for it is improper for a woman to speak in church. Was it from you that the word of God first went forth? Or has it come to you only? If anyone thinks he is a prophet or spiritual, let him recognize that the things which I write to you are the Lord's commandment. But if anyone does not recognize this, he is not recognized" (1 Corinthians 14:35-38).

Let us review some other familiar passages.

> Therefore I want the men in every place to pray, lifting up holy hands, without wrath or dissension. Likewise, I want women to adorn themselves with proper clothing, modestly and discreetly, not with braided hair or gold or pearls or costly garments, but rather by means of good works, as is proper for women making a claim to godliness. A woman must quietly receive instruction with entire submissiveness. But I do not allow a woman to teach or exercise authority over a man, but to remain quiet. For it was Adam who was first created, and then Eve. And it was not Adam who was deceived, but the woman being deceived, fell into transgression. But women will be preserved through the bearing of children if they continue in faith and love and sanctity with self-restraint (1 Timothy 2:8-15).

Paul's teaching is specific and consistent on this topic. It can be put together in harmony with other passages in which he expresses his admiration for his Christian sisters to show that this apostle understood that women have great value in the kingdom of God, but that it is God's plan for men to lead the assembly.

We know from our reading of the Gospels that Jesus intended women to have the equal access to His blood sacrifice that Galatians 3:28 describes. We have the example of His lengthy conversation with the Samaritan woman in John 4, His defense of the woman taken in adultery in John 8. We know about His love for the sisters of Lazarus, Martha and Mary. In Mark 16 we have the account of Jesus' resurrection and His appearance first to Mary Magdalene. In the book of Acts there are the accounts of the healing of Dorcas, the conversion of Lydia, and their good deeds, and of the sin of Sapphira. We also know of the work Priscilla did with her husband Aquilla as recorded first in Acts 18, where there is a record of them assisting Apollos to grow in his understanding of the gospel—a private conversation in which Priscilla participated. In Romans 16 in his personal greetings, Paul names specifically sixteen women who were greatly admired servants of the Lord and those who had been of great assistance to him. We also studied in the last chapter of his concern for the two sisters in the Philippian congregation. Anyone who would read all of these passages and would still maintain that Paul hated or demeaned his sisters in Christ, ought to reconsider whether she is truly reading the Word of God for what it says or possibly reading with an agenda planted there by those who are tools of Satan to degrade the church.

As we come to the end of this long lesson, let's go back to the passage in Galatians. Rather than understanding verse 28 of chapter 3 to mean that all people have equal access to salvation through Christ, these false teachers want to deny all male and female in the church. This is, of course, not consistent with the other types of people in the passage. The Jewish and Gentile cultures were not erased by this teaching, they came together in harmony by the grace of God. This verse did not erase the evil of slavery, either in the Roman Empire or in any other time; it made these people equal under the eyes of God. There are some dangerous consequences of attempting to remove all distinction of male and female in the church. It goes beyond what was written, which Paul warned against in 1 Corinthians 4:6. It allows the adherents to this philosophy to appoint female elders, saying that the Scriptures in Timothy and Titus were just referring to "older" people, and that instead of saying an elder is to be the husband of one wife, they can just substitute the word *spouse*. This leads to an even greater consequence. I believe this has not been considered by many ordinary Christians. In the throes of emotional highs exploring female-led churches, they fail to recognize that if there is no male or female in Christ, then marriage no longer must be between a man and a woman. This doctrine logically progresses to the point of insisting that congregations accept the membership of people who practice homosexual, bisexual, and transgender behavior without any teaching that they need to repent. Since Paul's doctrines are no longer to be taken at face value, except where the leaders of this movement decide they are, all of his teachings regarding these sexual behaviors can be swept away in an emotional tide of acceptance and compliance with the culture around us.

This chapter has been longer than the others because it is so important that we prepare ourselves to stand against these false teachings. If we are immersing ourselves in all of the challenging activities that are in need of our service, if we are focused on being loving teachers in our homes, our children's schools, our communities, and in Bible classes, little time remains in our lives for us to learn. Can we not gratefully and scripturally participate in the formal assembly and learn from the studies our brothers in Christ offer? Can we not follow the submissive example of our Lord in being servants in our congregations, subject to the authority of our brethren as Christ was obedient to the authority of His Father? What more value do our egos require than the value God placed upon us in His eternal plan for our salvation with Christ's sacrifice as stated in John 3:16? We must be prayerful and courageous in standing against the tide of those who want to make us feel valued, heard, and respected in ways that are not consistent with God's law or the teachings of the New Testament. Let us pass on to young women their value to God so they will not be swayed by this false teaching.

CHAPTER ELEVEN **Questions for Discussion**

1. Considering encouragements we have had in other lessons for appropriate activities for women, list all the ways a woman can spread the gospel without being a leader in the formal assembly of the church.
2. How can we help women avoid the trap of feeling like second-class citizens in the kingdom because they do not lead in the assembly?
3. Are there examples in the Bible that teach it is appropriate for us to fear the results of disobedience to the Creator of the universe? Discuss with the group.
4. How can an opinionated woman with a quiet husband avoid leading the church in a passive-aggressive way?
5. If we approach our God-given role in the formal assembly with joyful obedience, how will we assist younger women to understand its value?
6. Does the fact that we have more talent in some areas than some men mean that we should necessarily take over those areas?

References

1. Barton, Sara Gaston, 2012. A Woman Called; Piecing Together the Ministry Puzzle, Leafwood Publishers, Abilene, TX.

2. Halley's Bible Handbook, Twenty-Fourth Edition, Copyright 1965. Published by Zondervan Publishing House Grand Rapids, Michigan, by arrangement with Halley's Bible Handbook,® Inc.
3. Randolph, Robert M. (2003) "Why Women Should Be Preaching in the Churches of Christ," *Leaven*: Vol. 11: Iss. 4, Article 10. Available at http://digitalcommons.pepperdine.edu/leaven/vol11/iss4/10. Accessed December 10, 2014.
4. Ron White, December 2014, Sermons from 1 Corinthians 14 regarding organization of worship instructions.
5. https://search.yahoo.com/search?fr=mcafee&typevimeo.com" Meet Lauren King, Preaching Intern at the 4th avenue church of Christ." Accessed November 14, 2014. I copied the dialog of this video verbatim before it was removed from the Internet one week later. Another video, http://vimeo.com/114312987 "Woman Preacher at 4th Ave. church of Christ," accessed January 29, 2015 discusses the video and includes audio clips, validating my initial research.
6. http://www.truthmagazine.com/the-1990-freed-hardeman-preachers-forum-womens-role-... The 1990 Freed-Hardeman Preacher's Forum: Women's Role in the Church by Wayne Goforth, Accessed 12/10/2014.
7. "Scripture quotation is from The ESV Bible (Holy Bible, English Standard Version), copyright 2001 by Crossway, a publishing ministry of Good News Publishers. Used by permission. All rights reserved."

CHAPTER 12

Jesus, Hope of the Courageous

A review of recent world news stories includes airplane crashes, race riots, terrorist attacks, mass kidnappings, political upheaval, school shootings, imprisonment and persecution of minorities, disease epidemics, fires, floods, hurricanes, births, marriages, divorces, and suicides of celebrities. Among my friends and family members there are concerns over aging family members, serious illnesses, job losses, unexpected moves, births, weddings, divorces, funerals, car accidents, the list goes on. It probably sounds familiar because we all experience similar issues. In our study, readers have been asked to consider society decay in many areas. In the short-term, the outlook for modern society does not appear hopeful.

For the Christian to maintain hope is to go against prevailing attitudes. Where the love of God does not exist, there is only emptiness. Human laws have successfully removed God from public life, and efforts to remove Him from private life continue. The hole in society's collective soul has been filled with evolutionary philosophy, which leaves people with no purpose or guidance, believing they are no more than animals. Humanity lives with the consequences of this daily. Much of popular entertainment centers on dystopian scenarios where all that has supported a cohesive culture, innocence and trust of any kind, has been destroyed. The story with the happy ending is diluted with tragedy because generations of our people have experienced more tragedy than happiness. Daily life for many is a continual pursuit of more stuff for self, intense experiences for self, and engaging entertainment for self, for the purpose of generating more stuff, more experiences, and more entertainment. But a large part of society rejects this cycle in favor of a mentality that expresses intensifying anger and cynicism. This group intrudes on the other in the form of ongoing protests in hotbeds of violence or on social media in snarky comment strings and blogs.

As women courageous enough to recognize the decay in the world around us or experiencing the fallout from it personally, where do we find the hope to go on? Just as for the other issues we have raised in these studies, we will find the answers in the Bible, specifically in the New Testament. Mature readers will immediately point to readings such as the following:

> Blessed be the God and Father of our Lord Jesus Christ, who according to His great mercy has caused us to be born again to a living hope through the resurrection of Jesus Christ from the dead, to obtain an inheritance which is imperishable and undefiled and will not fade away, reserved in heaven for you, who are protected by the power of God through faith for a salvation ready to be revealed in the last time. In this you greatly rejoice, even though now for a little while, if necessary, you have been distressed by various trials, so that the proof of your faith, being more precious than gold which is perishable, even though tested by fire, may be found to result in praise and glory and honor at the revelation of Jesus Christ; and though you have not seen Him, you love Him, and though you do not see Him now, but believe in Him, you greatly rejoice with joy inexpressible and full of glory, obtaining as the outcome of your faith the salvation of your souls (1 Peter 1:3-9).

This passage and others like it written by the apostles display their great hope in Christ. What they learned from Jesus in the three years they were with Him made their faith strong enough that none of them denied their faith throughout their lives. Accounts of their lives by early historians assert that many of them died martyrs' deaths. Secular history records the deaths of others over the years for their belief in Jesus, and today in countries around the world, believers in Christ sit in prisons and face death for their faith. In this chapter we will first consider the eternal nature of God's plan to bring us into a peaceful unity with Him. Then, as we consider some things from the first four books of the New Testament, we can gain a basic understanding of the hope that the apostles had in Jesus.

To understand why we need to have hope, we must briefly go back to the beginning of mankind, in the Garden of Eden. We already covered the fall of man into sin. The serpent promised Eve great knowledge, and she and Adam received it. They understood immediately that they could not take back their rebellion. They could not on their own restore the perfect relationship they had with their Father. They could not take back the knowledge of their nakedness. The problem with sin is that no matter how good it feels at the time, we cannot take it back, cannot erase the scars that it leaves. As God spoke curses on the ground of the earth and the serpent and declared punishments on the man and the woman, there was the seed of hope. In this passage is the first prophecy of Christ, who would defeat evil.

> "And I will put enmity Between you and the woman, And between your seed and her seed; He shall bruise you on the head, And you shall bruise Him on the heel" (Genesis 3:15).

To understand the verse we need to know that the "He" being referred to is Christ. The word *bruise* means to crush. Satan did bring about Christ's death, crushing Him on the heel, but when God raised Christ from the dead He crushed Satan on the head—a decisive victory over the law of sin and death. This law was the elemental law from the beginning. In the Old Testament, with the creation of the Israelite nation through Abraham, Isaac, and

Jacob, God chose a people with whom to teach the world about the nature of sin and atonement. The Jewish people, through their cycles of faithfulness to the Law of Moses and sinful behavior, illustrated that mankind cannot on his own perfectly obey any law. The other purpose served by the Jewish nation was that through their genealogy would come the Messiah, Jesus Christ. People who choose to ignore study of the Old Testament cannot fully understand or appreciate the power of the gospel of Christ. People who believe the God of the Old Testament is not the same as the God of the New Testament have not read the history completely or choose not to recognize all of the ways God used to teach humanity about our need for Him.

In the New Testament, the apostle John begins his gospel with a bird's eye view of the eternal plan of God.

> In the beginning was the Word, and the Word was with God, and the Word was God. He was in the beginning with God. All things came into being through Him, and apart from Him nothing came into being that has come into being. In Him was life, and the life was the Light of men....And the Word became flesh, and dwelt among us, and we saw His glory, glory as of the only begotten from the Father, full of grace and truth (John 1:1-4, 14).

In this passage, the Greek word *logos*, which is translated "word" refers to Divine Expression.[1] It is used to describe Jesus' function as the exact representation of God. The writer of the letter to the Hebrews uses this imagery as well:

> God, after He spoke long ago to the fathers in the prophets in many portions and in many ways, in these last days has spoken to us in His Son, whom He appointed heir of all things, through whom also He made the world. And He is the radiance of His glory and the exact representation of His nature, and upholds all things by the word of His power (Hebrews 1:1-3).

The Apostle Paul also describes God's plan for the rescue of mankind from sin in his letter to the Colossian Christians:

> ...giving thanks to the Father, who has qualified us to share in the inheritance of the saints in Light. For He (*God*) rescued us from the domain of darkness, and transferred us to the kingdom of His beloved Son, in whom we have redemption, the forgiveness of sins. He (*Jesus*) is the image of the invisible God, the firstborn of all creation. For by Him all things were created, both in the heavens and on the earth, visible and invisible, whether thrones or dominions or rulers or authorities—all things have been created through Him and for Him. He is before all things, and in Him all things hold together. He is also the head of the body, the church; and He is the beginning, the firstborn from the dead, so that He Himself will come to have first place in everything (Colossians 1:12-18, italics mine).

These passages help the seeker of God's truth to understand that Jesus existed from the beginning of time in equality and unity with God the Father. Jesus was active in God's creation of the universe. From this perfect beginning it was God's plan to restore sinful humanity to Himself through Jesus. The following verses describe Jesus' role as Savior even more specifically:

> Have this attitude in yourselves which was also in Christ Jesus, who, although He existed in the form of God, did not regard equality with God a thing to be grasped, but emptied Himself taking the form of a bond-servant, and being made in the likeness of men. Being found in appearance as a man, He humbled Himself by becoming obedient to the point of death, even death on a cross. For this reason also, God highly exalted Him, and bestowed on Him the name which is above every name, so that at the name of Jesus EVERY KNEE WILL BOW, of those who are in heaven and on earth and under the earth, and that every tongue will confess that Jesus Christ is Lord, to the glory of God the Father (Philippians 2:5-11).

The first four books of the New Testament are called Gospels because they tell the good news of Jesus' life and teachings on this earth, as well as the accounts of His death on the cross and His resurrection. Through the accounts of four different men, we read their different perspectives written on most of the same highlights of Jesus' life and teachings. Matthew's gospel, addressed primarily to the Jews, emphasizes throughout how Jesus' life fulfilled the prophecies made throughout Jewish history. Many readers tend to skip over the first chapter, a genealogy of Jesus' ancestry, back to Adam. This chapter is important, however, in proving the eternal nature of God's plan, and readers of the time would have recognized all of the names. Matthew records detailed teachings, such as those commonly called the Sermon on the Mount in chapters five, six, and seven, as well as many conversations Jesus had with his followers as He taught them and led them to understanding of the eternal nature of His work. In the following exchange with Peter, we are exposed to one highlight of their growth:

> He said to them, "But who do you say that I am?" Simon Peter answered, "You are the Christ, the Son of the living God." And Jesus said to him, "Blessed are you, Simon Barjona, because flesh and blood did not reveal this to you, but My Father who is in heaven" (Matthew 16:15-17).

Teaching His followers about the serving nature of His Kingdom was an important part of Jesus' training of His apostles, because like all of us, they tended to get caught up in status and authority.

> But Jesus called them to Himself and said, "You know that the rulers of the Gentiles lord it over them, and their great men exercise authority over them. It is not this way among you, but whoever wishes to become great among you shall be your servant, and whoever wishes to be first among you shall be your slave; just as the Son of Man did not come to be served, but to serve, and to give His life a ransom for many" (Matthew 20:25-28).

We have considered several ways we as women can imitate our Lord in service in the communities in which we live, in our families, and in our churches. There is a common thread in all of them, a thread of putting others first, of giving of ourselves in willingness to do undesirable tasks. There is no fame or glamour in doing many of the things that need doing in spreading the love and truth of Jesus to this world. Our work will be marginalized, and sometimes we will find ourselves being ridiculed or threatened by those whose status or power is threatened by the Word of God; but as we experience these things we are following in the steps of our Lord who experienced them first.

In the short gospel of Mark is a perspective of Jesus as a Lord who knew He did not have long on this earth to accomplish His ministry. With the word *immediately*, which is used several times in the book, we get a sense of urgency and focus on the part of Jesus. The miracles Mark describes for the reader bring credibility to the message preached. The hope of physical healings realized by followers of Jesus was intended to lead them to a stronger hope of spiritual healing through obedience. As more of the population came to believe in and follow Jesus, He came to the attention quickly of the religious rulers of the time, the Pharisees and Sadducees. They repeatedly tried to invalidate His teachings with criticisms and testing questions, but He never shrank from answering them. Observe in the following passage how His answer reveals their lack of understanding regarding spiritual things.

> Jesus said to them, "Is this not the reason you are mistaken, that you do not understand the Scriptures or the power of God? For when they rise from the dead, they neither marry nor are given in marriage, but are like the angels in heaven. But regarding the fact that the dead rise again, have you not read in the book of Moses, in the passage about the burning bush, how God spoke to him, saying, 'I AM THE GOD OF ABRAHAM AND THE GOD OF ISAAC, and the God of Jacob'? He is not the God of the dead, but of the living; you are greatly mistaken" (Mark 12:24-27).

Jesus' compassion for the downtrodden people was exemplified in all of His work, but a special account revealed the value He placed on any love offered to Him. He honored the service this poor, imperfect woman offered Him. This passage reminds us that God sees the sincere offerings of love we make, even though our hearts and lives are tainted by sin. This gives us hope.

> While He was in Bethany at the home of Simon the leper, and reclining at the table, there came a woman with an alabaster vial of very costly perfume of pure nard; and she broke the vial and poured it over His head. But some were indignantly remarking to one another, "Why has this perfume been wasted? For this perfume might have been sold for over three hundred denarii and the money given to the poor." And they were scolding her. But Jesus said, "Let her alone; why do you bother her? She has done a good deed to Me. For you always have the poor with you, and whenever you wish you can do good to them; but you do not always have Me. She has done what she could; she has anointed My body beforehand for the burial. Truly I say to you, wherever the gospel is preached in the whole world, what this woman has done will also be spoken of in memory of her" (Mark 14:3-9).

In the book of Luke we have the orderly report of a physician, the first of two books he wrote to a man named Theophilus. This is the only gospel specifically written to one person. However, we find in its comprehensive, detailed reporting a vivid picture of Jesus' teaching, interactions with His followers as well as His detractors, His love for mankind, and His determination to carry through with the sacrifice required of Him. The book would have appealed to Jews and Gentiles, as it included prophecies, doctrines, and accounts of Jesus' interactions with the Jews as He strove to get them to understand who He was. Luke recorded the account of the prodigal son in chapter fifteen of this book. This is a graphic demonstration of how our heavenly, eternal Father earnestly desires each one of us to return to Him. Today, as it has always been, people try so hard to invent their own lives, their own purpose based on their own desires, their own moral code. Some have never heard the gospel, and others, having heard, focus on what they perceive as restrictions, unwilling to trust that their Creator has their best interests at heart with His commands. In this account we see how Our Father gives every soul the choice to obey or reject His laws, then anxiously waits for those who will learn from life and return to Him. The only requirement, the simple but difficult thing, is to lay aside our pride and sin, to repent and submit to the Father. Once that is done, we are each welcomed back with open arms and celebrating. We are given every advantage and free access to the Father. Once we enjoy the blessings of harmony with the Father, it is up to us to be on guard against being the suspicious, jealous elder brother in the account. As we have been fully accepted back simply because of our repentance, even though that repentance is imperfect, it is our place to celebrate and welcome others with the same love we have received.

One unique feature of the book of Luke is the detailed report of Jesus' conversation with Cleopas and another brother as they traveled from Jerusalem to Emmaus on the third day after his crucifixion. This appears to be one of only two conversations recorded that Jesus had with disciples who were not apostles after His resurrection, the other being His conversation with Mary at the tomb. We can read of Jesus' conversation with the men in the long account in Luke 24:13-35. In verse 21, as they were relating the events of previous days to Jesus without recognizing Him, they relayed how they had hoped He would redeem Israel from Roman occupation and how sad they were. Luke recorded Jesus took the opportunity to reveal to them the true purpose of His work. After He left them, they exclaimed about the encounter,

> "Were not our hearts burning within us while He was speaking to us on the road, while He was explaining the Scriptures to us?" (Luke 24:32)

Their emotions were stirred by Jesus' speaking, but it was the understanding of the Scriptures that gave them true hope.

As was mentioned earlier in this study, John seems to have written his gospel with an eternal perspective. As a young apostle, he and his brother James were given the name "Sons of Thunder," noted in Mark 3:17. This may have been fulfilled when the two of them volunteered to call down fire from heaven on unbelievers in Samaria, recorded in Luke 9:54. But this John is the same one who wrote the three epistles by his name at the end of the New Testament. John records in his gospel the teachings Jesus gave his Apostles on the night He was betrayed. He allows us to experience the intimate, loving words Jesus had to say to friends He knew He was leaving, but who did not completely understand what was about to happen.

> "I will not leave you as orphans; I will come to you. After a little while the world will no longer see Me, but you will see Me; because I live, you will live also. In that day you will know that I am in My Father, and you in Me, and I in you...These things I have spoken to you while abiding with you. But the Helper, the Holy Spirit, whom the Father will send in My name, He will teach you all things, and bring to your remembrance all that I said to you. Peace I leave with you; My peace I give to you; not as the world gives do I give to you. Do not let your heart be troubled, nor let it be fearful" (John 14:18-20, 25-27).

> "This I command you, that you love one another. If the world hates you, you know that it has hated Me before it hated you. If you were of the world, the world would love its own; but because you are not of the world, but I chose you out of the world, because of this the world hates you" (John 15:17-19).

> "These things I have spoken to you, so that in Me you may have peace. In the world you have tribulation, but take courage; I have overcome the world" (John 16:33).

In the three years that Jesus' apostles walked and talked and lived with Him, these twelve men saw wondrous signs and learned to trust Him. In spite of those wondrous privileges, Judas still chose to betray Jesus, in a terrible moment of bad judgment from which he did not recover. Peter's fledgling faith failed him at the crisis point, and he denied Jesus three times. But Peter was able to humble himself and repent, a great example to all of us prodigals who have to humble ourselves and repent periodically during our Christian walk. Once filled with the Holy Spirit on the Day of Pentecost, these twelve men lit the world on fire figuratively, spreading the gospel with earnest focus to everyone they met. None of these apostles ever recanted. What they saw and experienced gave them hope to courageously face prison and torture and martyrs' deaths. Their teaching has been powerful enough to reach down through the ages to us in the twenty-first century. The Lord has protected His Word through the centuries against tyrants who would have destroyed it, martyrs and secret survivors handing it down.

Paul, the former persecutor of Christians, met Christ on the Damascus road and was transformed into an obedient servant, inspired to write most of the epistles of the New Testament. He wrote of the hope of the courageous Christian in many passages. Consider these verses:

> Therefore, having been justified by faith, we have peace with God through our Lord Jesus Christ, through whom also we have obtained our introduction by faith into this grace in which we stand; and we exult in the hope of the glory of God. And not only this, but we also exult in our tribulations, knowing that tribulation brings about perseverance; and perseverance, proven character; and proven character, hope; and hope does not disappoint, because the love of God has been poured out within our hearts through the Holy Spirit who was given to us (Romans 5:1-5).

Paul believed that as Christians engaged in obedient, active faith we would achieve peace with the God of the universe. What a blessing! In this world of troubles, we have the answer to peace! In spite of our failings, our sins, we stand in God's grace, thanks to the sacrifice of Jesus. We learn to perceive our troubles and struggles with temptation as opportunities to grow more like Christ in attitude and service. And we have hope. But our hope is not in this world, just as Jesus told Pilate that His kingdom was not of this world in John 18:36. In Romans 8 Paul shares how our hope is in things not seen. In verse 18 he exclaims, "For I consider that the sufferings of this present time are not worthy to be compared with the glory that is to be revealed to us." He expands on the concept of hope later in the same chapter. Reflect on these words to the Roman Christians:

> For in hope we have been saved, but hope that is seen is not hope; for who hopes for what he already sees? But if we hope for what we do not see, with perseverance we wait eagerly for it…Who will separate us from the love of Christ? Will tribulation, or distress, or persecution, or famine, or nakedness, or peril, or sword? Just as it is written, "FOR YOUR SAKE WE ARE BEING PUT TO DEATH ALL DAY LONG; WE WERE CONSIDERED AS SHEEP TO BE SLAUGHTERED." But in all these things we overwhelmingly conquer through Him who loved us. For I am convinced that neither death, nor life, nor angels, nor principalities, nor things present, nor things to come, nor powers, nor height, nor depth, nor any other created thing, will be able to separate us from the love of God, which is in Christ Jesus our Lord (Romans 8:24-25, 35-39).

In the letter to the Hebrew Christians, the writer defined faith as, "the assurance of things hoped for" in Hebrews 11:1. The Greek word for hope means "favorable and confident expectation, a forward look with assurance".[1] The Hebrew writer shared Paul's unshakable hope. The accounts of courageous obedience to God in Hebrews 11, by people who died without seeing the final hope fulfilled in Christ, are there for us to read. Our own faith and hope can be strengthened by these examples.

I hope revisiting the Gospel accounts of Jesus' life and teachings, and consideration of the faith of the Apostles has empowered you to commit to living a more deliberate, courageous life of service to the Lord. My experience has been that as we focus more on the reality of the Word of God, depend on its truth, and attempt to live out the commands of God in our lives, He blesses us with stronger faith. This in turn helps us to focus spiritually even more, depend on Him even more, and live the cycle more and more effectively. Rather than a hope for Utopia on earth, our hope is for the paradise of eternal life with our Heavenly Father. We treasure the blessings of this life, but long for the next.

I leave you with a final set of verses. These are the ones I asked my husband to read to me when I learned of my sister Danna's sudden death fourteen years ago. The image of heaven depicted here became real to me, and my hope of being at home with the Lord and her one day became almost a tangible thing as he read these words.

> Then I saw a new heaven and a new earth; for the first heaven and the first earth passed away, and there is no longer any sea. And I saw the holy city, new Jerusalem, coming down out of heaven from God, made ready as a bride adorned for her husband. And I heard a loud voice from the throne, saying, "Behold, the tabernacle of God is among men, and He will dwell among them, and they shall be His people, and God Himself will be among them, and He will wipe away every tear from their eyes; and there will no longer be any death; there will no longer be any mourning, or crying, or pain; the first things have passed away." And He who sits on the throne said, "Behold, I am making all things new." And He said, "Write, for these words are faithful and true." Then He said to me, "It is done. I am the Alpha and the Omega, the beginning and the end. I will give to the one who thirsts from the spring of the water of life without cost. He who overcomes will inherit these things, and I will be his God and he will be My son" (Revelation 21:1-7).

CHAPTER TWELVE **Questions for Discussion**

1. How does your hope for eternal life with God affect your thoughts and actions every day?
2. In times of sorrow or trial are there specific verses you go to in order to keep up hope? Share them with the group.
3. As children we used to memorize Bible verses. How would memorizing Bible passages about our hope be of help to you if you could not access your Bible?
4. Share with the group any songs that remind you of your hope.
5. After this study, can you explain how living your Christian life daily can help bring hope to your community?

Reference

1. Strong, James, 2010. The New Strong's Expanded Exhaustive Concordance of the Bible. Published by Thomas Nelson Publishers, Nashville, TN.w

www.ingramcontent.com/pod-product-compliance
Lightning Source LLC
LaVergne TN
LVHW051600070426
835507LV00021B/2674